"The Boxer" (Simon and Garfunkel)
"You've Made Me So Very Happy" (Blood, Sweat & Tears)

Novels

1960

Rabbit, Run John Updike
Clea Lawrence Durrell
To Kill a Mockingbird Harper Lee; Pulitzer 1961
The Loneliness of the Long Distance Runner Alan Sillitoe
The Sotweed Factor John Barth
Absolute Beginners Colin MacInnes; pub. UK, 1959
The Violent Bear It Away Flannery O'Connor
A Separate Peace John Knowles
Facial Justice L. P. Hartley

1961

Franny and Zooey J. D. Salinger
Tropic of Cancer Henry Miller; pub. Paris, 1934
Catch-22 Joseph Heller
The Moviegoer Walker Percy
Revolutionary Road Richard Yates
Stranger in a Strange Land Robert Heinlein
A Burnt-Out Case Graham Greene
The Mighty and Their Fall Ivy Compton-Burnett
The Old Men at the Zoo Angus Wilson
The Winter of Our Discontent John Steinbeck
The Prime of Miss Jean Brodie Muriel Spark
The Carpetbaggers Harold Robbins

1962

One Flew Over the Cuckoo's Nest Ken Kesey
Another Country James Baldwin
Pale Fire Vladimir Nabokov
One Day in the Life of Ivan Denisovich Aleksandr Solzhenitsyn
The Ticket that Exploded William Burroughs
Letting Go Phillip Roth
The Reivers William Faulkner; Pulitzer 1963
Stern Bruce Jay Friedman
The Thin Red Line James Jones
Ship of Fools Katherine Anne Porter
Island Aldous Huxley
The Golden Notebook Doris Lessing
Big Sur Jack Kerouac

1963

V Thomas Pynchon
The Bell Jar Sylvia Plath
The Group Mary McCarthy
The Spy Who Came In from the Cold John Le Carre
The Tin Drum Gunter Grass
The Girls of Slender Means Muriel Spark
Rayuela Julio Cortazar; trans. as Hopscotch, 1966
The Centaur John Updike
The Unicorn Iris Murdoch
Run River Joan Didion

1964

Herzog Saul Bellow
The Wapshot Scandal John Cheever
Last Exit to Brooklyn Hubert Selby, Jr.
The Spire William Golding
A Single Man Christopher Isherwood
Julian Gore Vidal
Candy Terry Southern & Mason Hoffenberg; pub. Paris, 1958
Sometimes a Great Notion Ken Kesey
A Confederate General from Big Sur Richard Brautigan

Time of Silence Luis Martin-Santos
The Death of Artemio Cruz Carlos Fuentes

1965

An American Dream Norman Mailer
The Lockwood Concern John O'Hara
The Keepers of the House Shirley Ann Grau; Pulitzer
Dune Frank Herbert
The Ginger Man J. P. Donleavy; pub. Paris, 1955
The Painted Bird Jerzy Kosinski
The Man with the Golden Gun Ian Fleming

1966

In Cold Blood Truman Capote
The Fixer Bernard Malamud; Pulitzer 1967
The Anti-Death League Kingsley Amis
Wide Sargasso Sea Jean Rhys
Valley of the Dolls Jacqueline Susann
Been Down So Long It Looks Like Up to Me Richard Fariña
The Time of the Angels Iris Murdoch
The Comedians Graham Greene
Giles Goat-Boy John Barth
The Late Bourgeois World Nadine Gordimer

1967

The Confessions of Nat Turner William Styron; Pulitzer, 1968
The Manor Isaac Bashevis Singer
Diary of a Mad Housewife Sue Kaufman
Why Are We in Vietnam? Norman Mailer
Death Kit Susan Sontag
The Free-Lance Pallbearers Ismael Reed
The Public Burning Robert Coover
The Vendor of Sweets R. K. Narayan
The Outsiders S. E. Hinton
Snow White Donald Barthelme

1968

Myra Breckinridge Gore Vidal
Armies of the Night Norman Mailer
True Grit Charles Portis
House Made of Dawn N. Scott Momaday; Pulitzer, 1969
Couples John Updike
The Sporting Club Thomas McGuane
A Fan's Notes Frederick Exley
The Image Men J. B. Priestley

1969

Slaughterhouse Five Kurt Vonnegut
Portnoy's Complaint Phillip Roth
Ada Vladimir Nabokov
The French Lieutenant's Woman John Fowles
The Godfather Mario Puzo
Naked Came the Stranger Pornographic satire, 24 authors
The Bluest Eye Toni Morrison
Them Joyce Carol Oates
The Left Hand of Darkness Ursula K. LeGuin
Mrs. Eckdorf in O'Neill's Hotel William Trevor

Movies

1960

Psycho Alfred Hitchcock
L'Aventura Michelangelo Antonioni
Spartacus Stanley Kubrick
The Apartment Billy Wilder
Saturday Night and Sunday Morning Karel Reisz
Hiroshima, Mon Amour Alain Resnais
The Entertainer Tony Richardson
The Virgin Spring Ingmar Bergman
Rocco and His Brothers Luchino Visconti
The Magnificent Seven John Sturges
Shadows John Cassavetes
Our Man in Havana Carol Reed

1961

Breakfast at Tiffany's Blake Edwards
Jules et Jim François Truffaut
West Side Story Jerome Robbins
La Dolce Vita Federico Fellini
Breathless Jean-Luc Godard
The Hustler Robert Rossen
Never On Sunday Jules Dassin
A Taste of Honey Tony Richardson
Judgment at Nuremberg Stanley Kramer
One-Eyed Jacks Marlon Brando
The Guns of Navarone J. Lee Thompson
Two Women Vittorio De Sica

1962

Lawrence of Arabia David Lean
The Manchurian Candidate John Frankenheimer
Divorce, Italian Style Pietro Germi
Lolita Stanley Kubrick
Long Day's Journey into Night Sidney Lumet
Through a Glass Darkly Ingmar Bergman
Last Year at Marienbad Alain Resnais
Whatever Happened to Baby Jane? Robert Aldrich
The Man Who Shot Liberty Valance John Ford
Gypsy Mervyn LeRoy
Advise and Consent Otto Preminger
The Miracle Worker Arthur Penn

1963

Hud Martin Ritt
8½ Federico Fellini
Tom Jones Tony Richardson
The Silence Ingmar Bergman
Cleopatra Joseph L. Mankiewicz
Irma La Douce Billy Wilder
The Birds Alfred Hitchcock
The Leopard Luchino Visconti
David and Lisa Frank Perry
The Trial Orson Welles

1964

Dr. Strangelove, or: How I Learned to Stop Worrying and Love the Bomb Stanley Kubrick
My Fair Lady George Cukor
A Hard Day's Night Richard Lester
Zorba the Greek Michael Cacoyannis
Lord of the Flies Peter Brook
Before the Revolution Bernardo Bertolucci
Becket Peter Glenville
Mary Poppins Robert Stevenson
Seance on a Wet Afternoon Bryan Forbes

1965

The Sound of Music Robert Wise
What's New, Pussycat? Clive Donner
Cul-de-sac Roman Polanski
Juliet of the Spirits Federico Fellini
Thunderball Terence Young
The Married Woman Jean-Luc Godard
Help! Richard Lester
A Thousand Clowns Fred Coe
The Spy Who Came In from the Cold Martin Ritt

Cat Ballou Elliot Silverstein
Othello Laurence Olivier

... Mike Nichols
The Battle of Algiers Gillo Pontecorvo
Georgy Girl Silvio Narizzano
Fahrenheit 451 François Truffaut
Modesty Blaise Joseph Losey
Alfie Lewis Gilbert
A Man for All Seasons Fred Zinneman
The Russians Are Coming! The Russians Are Coming! Norman Jewison
Persona Ingmar Bergman
A Man and a Woman Claude Lelouch
The Bible John Huston
Masculin-Feminin Jean-Luc Godard

1967

The Graduate Mike Nichols
Bonnie and Clyde Arthur Penn
Guess Who's Coming to Dinner Stanley Kramer
Cool Hanc Luke Stuart Rosenberg
In the Heat of the Night Norman Jewison
Belle de Jour Luis Buñuel
The Chelsea Girls Andy Warhol
Elvira Macigan Bo Widerberg
Thoroughly Modern Millie George Roy Hill
The Dirty Dozen Robert Aldrich
Ulysses Joseph Strick
In Cold Blood Richard Brooks
Up the Down Staircase Robert Mulligan

1968

2001: A Space Odyssey Stanley Kubrick
Rosemary's Baby Roman Polanski
The Green Berets John Wayne & Ray Kellogg
Petulia Richard Lester
Night of the Living Dead George Romero
Pretty Poison Noel Black
Bullitt Peter Yates
Oliver! Carol Reed
The Comedians Peter Glenville
Planet of the Apes Franklin J. Schaffner
Funny Girl William Wyler
The Killing of Sister George Aldrich
The Lion in Winter Anthony Harvey
Rachel, Rachel Paul Newman

1969

Easy Rider Dennis Hopper
Midnight Cowboy John Schlesinger
If... Lindsay Anderson
Butch Cassidy and the Sundance Kid George Roy Hill
Satyricon Federico Fellini
They Shoot Horses, Don't They? Sidney Pollack
I Am Curious (Yellow) Vilgot Sjoman
Z Costa-Gavras
Alice's Restaurant Arthur Penn
Bob and Carol and Ted and Alice Paul Mazursky
Take the Money and Run Woody Allen
Women in Love Ken Russell
Oh! What a Lovely War Richard Attenborough
The Damned Luchino Visconti
The Wild Bunch Sam Peckinpah
Last Summer Frank Perry
Once Upon a Time in the West Sergio Leone
Goodbye, Columbus Larry Peerce

THE 60s

THE 60s

MALLARD
PRESS

A FRIEDMAN GROUP BOOK

Published by MALLARD PRESS
An Imprint of BDD Promotional Book Company, Inc.
666 Fifth Avenue
New York, N.Y. 10103

Mallard Press and the accompanying duck logo are registered trademarks of
BDD Promotional Book Co., Inc. registered in the U.S. Patent and Trademark Office.

ISBN 0-7924-5764-1

THE 60s
was prepared and produced by
Michael Friedman Publishing Group, Inc.
15 West 26th Street
New York, New York 10010

Editor: Sharyn Rosart
Art Direction and Design: Devorah Levinrad
Layout: Maria Avitabile
Photography Editor: Daniella Jo Nilva

Grateful acknowledgement is given to authors, publishers, and photographers for permission to reprint material.
Every effort has been made to determine copyright owners. In the case of any omissions, the publishers will be
pleased to make suitable acknowledgements in future editions.

Typeset by Classic Type, Inc.
Color separations by Colourmatch Graphic Equipment & Services
Printed and bound in Hong Kong by Leefung-Asco Printers Ltd.

Additional Photo Credits
© Jason Lauré: pp. 6, 10–11, 42–43, 74–75, 96–97
© World Wide Photos: pp. 16–17, 36–37

DEDICATION

To my parents

ACKNOWLEDGEMENTS

This book, or much else, would never have been written without the inconceivably patient support of my father. I'd also like to thank Michael and Donna, for putting up with me.

CONTENTS

Introduction

◆

page 8

Chapter One

◆

WORLD EVENTS

page 10

Chapter Two

◆

PROTEST

page 42

Chapter Three

◆

ARTS and ENTERTAINMENT

page 74

Chapter Four

◆

LIFESTYLES

page 96

BIBLIOGRAPHY

◆

page 117

INDEX

◆

page 118

Introduction

Not too many years ago I sat in the library of my fraternity house, looking through some old college yearbooks. The 1969–70 edition was especially arresting. In the seniors' section—where the students' photos are larger than those of underclassmen and each individual is permitted extra space for a bit of *curriculum vitae* (e.g., "Gunnar Pelle Torkelsen…'the Tork'…'Swede'…QUOTE: 'We may never pass this way again.'—Seals & Crofts" etc.)—each lucky senior was the beneficiary of an entire page on which, in a pleasingly arty fashion, he or she arranged soulful impressionistic photos, peace signs, snatches of his or her own *vers libre*, and favorite quotes from the likes of Arthur Rimbaud, Albert Camus, and Simone de Beauvoir (rendered in the original French).

One such page gave me special pause: it featured a grainy black-and-white photo of a pretty young woman—wearing beads, bellbottoms, and, I think, a Hopi headband—perched atop the hood of a VW Beetle, a flurry of autumnal leaves floating in front of her face. Beneath the photo appeared a bit of verse, part of which, oddly enough, I remember almost verbatim:

> …Rose remnants of a time since gone
> Not this barbarian age of Nixon and napalm
> And bilked blacks whose hope is the Gun.
> Was it thus then, or was it not?

Plus ca change, plus c'est la meme chose.

Where is she now? I had to wonder.

Eventually I turned to the "Greek" section to check the composite photograph of my own fraternity—curious as to whether they, too, had felt the urge to set down for posterity some lyrical, collectively disenchanted *pensée*. But no; instead, under the heading "Frat Chat," there were the usual notes about a year well and merrily spent and, as ever, a few words of patronizing condolence for the "house-mom," a Mrs. Thayer (whose haggard countenance stared out from

the center of the composite), who had managed "once again" to keep the "good ship Sig" on course—no mean feat, apparently.

Nor was there anything remotely radical-looking about this group: their hairstyles were uniform, as if all clipped by the same meticulous barber (himself a Nixon man), and their blue blazers—I noted with a strange thrill—were but the same blazer, passed from one to the other as each took his place before the camera. A hasty back-and-forth check confirmed that none of my distant brethren had opted to partake of the poignant pastiches in the seniors' section. Indeed, the sole effect of the turbulent Sixties on this

lapidary bunch was, if anything, a certain thinning of the ranks, down from the usual fifty-or-so members to maybe twenty. But how proudly, how serenely aloof these twenty were to the times, however a-changin'. They all smirked, as if in drunken recognition of this fact.

A campus, a world divided, forsooth! I closed the dusty lid of that yearbook and pondered a crucial question: if I had been born, say, fifteen years earlier, and had thus come of age in the Sixties, what choice would I have made for myself? Would I have donned that emblematic blue blazer, heedless to the Winds of Change? Or would I have been among those who affirmed, with the prophet Bob, that "There's a battle outside and it's ragin'/It'll soon shake your windows and rattle your walls"? Would I have eschewed banal campus high jinks and become part of the utopian "Love Generation," dressed for Aquarius in my counter-cultural livery of sandals, tunic, beads, and headband (or nothing at all)? How many of my generation have not, in sober retrospection, wondered as much?

But the Sixties, of course, were years of variously mutating modes, and one was not limited to a stark choice between the beads or the blazer. There was upheaval, yes, but there was also affluence, which meant that middle- and upper-class youngsters, subsidized by parents whom they loathed, could afford to experiment, searching in leisure for the lifestyle that most suited their particular inner needs. In moments of high whimsy, I fancy myself as sampling the entire spectrum of Sixties personae: as the decade begins, I drop out of school and join a flock of activist folksingers, all of us hopping freightcars southward to join the civil rights movement, help rebuild burned and bombed-out churches, attend sit-ins, and get hit on the head until, with the British Invasion, I buy a Beatles wig and go on a pilgrimage to London, making the mod scene and even glimpsing Mick once or twice in Chelsea until, swept along with the vast tide of swinging youth, I find myself in San Francisco, enclosed behind a dank mop of hair as I ponder Oneness on a stoop in the Haight until, after one mind-bending trip too many, I inadvertently become a Hare Krishna, chanting George Harrison songs in the park until riot-police on their way to a protest pause to club me over my newly-shaven pate....

Finally, I imagine finding myself much as I am now—my hair growing back to medium length, my tunic shucked for a well-starched Brooks Brothers shirt, happily reunited with wary parents. Perhaps we'd end up watching the moonwalk together, and I'd sit there musing over the moon's metaphoric significance, recalling a T. S. Eliot quote that I'd read once in some yearbook: "We shall not cease from exploration and the end of all our exploring will be to arrive where we started and know the place for the first time."

◆ CHAPTER ONE ◆
WORLD
EVENTS

The Cold War

"Whether you like it or not," Soviet premier Nikita Khruschev told United Nations ambassadors in 1959, "history is on our side. We will bury you."

In the early Sixties, war between the superpowers often seemed more likely to occur than not. With postwar territorial gains, the Soviet sphere of influence had increased significantly, with alien and submissive populations totalling 134,188,000. Then the "iron curtain" descended, cutting off Soviet Russia and her satellites from the rest of the world. Soviet leaders justified such measures (encroachment and brutal consolidation) in the name of historical inevitability: "We are convinced that sooner or later capitalism will perish," Khruschev said, "just as feudalism perished earlier.…All the world will come to Communism. History does not ask whether you want it or not."

In the meantime, it was the policy of the Soviet Union to nudge "history" at every opportunity. In 1956, Soviets flouted international law with the invasion of Hungary, undaunted by the censure of the United Nations. A shaky (and doomed) alliance was formed with Red China, with both countries sponsoring guerilla campaigns in Indochina and throughout the Third World, where the West had relinquished its sovereignty through sweeping de-colonization.

As the Sixties began, relations between East and West had deteriorated catastrophically, with conflict seeming imminent over crises in Cuba and Berlin: the United States had severed relations with Castro's regime in 1959, driving Cuba over to the Soviets, and thus giving the latter a crucial foothold in the Western Hemisphere; and Soviets were demanding the removal of NATO troops from Berlin, which would effectively leave the city, a Western outpost in Communist Eastern Europe, at the Soviets' mercy.

Threats of nuclear assault were flung around on both sides with incredible recklessness, despite the deterrent of mutually assured destruction. Though in fact the United States enjoyed an estimated ten-to-one advantage in strategic strike capability, warhawks in the Pentagon stoked national hysteria with rumors of a "missile gap," thereby justifying escalated defense spending throughout the Fifties and into the Sixties. On August 14, 1958 Senator Kennedy compared the supposed loss of America's "superiority in nuclear striking power" to England's loss, in the sixteenth century, of Calais, her last stronghold on the continent. Waxing Churchillian, Kennedy declaimed: "Why cannot we realize that the coming years of the gap present us with a peril more deadly than any wartime danger we have ever known?…Come then—let us to the task, to the battle, and the toil—each to our part, each to our station.…"

Whatever his liberalism in other matters, Kennedy was well right-of-center where the Soviet Union was concerned. (Though later, having thwarted the Soviets in the Cuban Missile Crisis, Kennedy would smile at cabinet members and say: "Whoever believed in a 'missile gap' anyway?")

From 1956 to 1960, the United States sent U-2 reconnaissance planes out of Incirlik Air Force Base in Turkey to photograph missile sites within the Soviet Union. The U-2s flew at an altitude thought to be beyond the range of Soviet planes and antiaircraft missiles. When one such flight went down over the city of Sverdlovsk on May 1, 1960, the United States, assuming the pilot had been killed in the crash, claimed the U-2 had violated Soviet airspace by accident, and that no espionage had been committed. Then the Soviets sprung their trap: the U-2 pilot, Francis Gary Powers, had survived and made a full confession.

The United States had good reason to believe that Powers was dead, even apart from the reasonable surmise that he'd be killed once the plane was hit. Before his flight, Powers had been given a silver dollar concealing a poison pin, with the suggestion that, if captured, he should kill himself rather than try to withstand torture. Powers remembers the decision he made after his plane was destroyed, during the long parachute drop that followed:

"I opened the silver dollar and took the pin out and threw the coin away. I looked at the needle—and to this day I don't know why I didn't use it. I almost did. I was so afraid of the complete unknown, and I was thinking, 'The worst things that can happen to a person are what they're going to do to me.' I really, seriously considered it, and I don't know why I didn't use it. I guess it was just 'Wait and see what happens.'"

What happened was this: Powers was tried in Moscow and sentenced to ten years in prison for spying on the Soviet Union (he was later exchanged for Rudolf Abel, a Soviet agent); and at the Paris summit conference two weeks later, Khruschev denounced the Eisenhower administration for "crudely flouting the universally accepted standards of international law and the lofty principles of the United Nations Charter." He then walked out on the talks, having added that the United States president would not be welcome in the Soviet Union the following month, when further meetings had been planned.

"[The Soviet Union] cannot be among the participants in negotiations where one [country] has made treachery the basis of [its] policy," he said. "Let the disgrace and responsibility for this rest with those who have proclaimed a bandit policy toward the Soviet Union."

In a New York Times commentary, James Reston wrote: "The general reaction in Paris…was that the situation was not as bad as it looked, for the simple, logical reason that nothing could be quite that bad."

On taking office in 1961, President Kennedy sent a note to Khruschev that read in part: "Free people do not accept the claim of historical inevitability for the communist revolution….The great revolution in the history of man, past, present and future, is the revolution of those determined to be free."

The Soviets' ideological surety—Khruschev's conviction that war between East and West was inevitable and that communism was bound to triumph—made the prospect of peaceful coexistence seem all but unattainable. In the West, there was a growing, desperate sense that a "worldwide revolution" was actually in progress, and that perhaps the doctrine of its "inevitable" success was to some degree valid.

Archive Photos

There was much talk of the so-called "domino effect"—as one country fell to communism, its neighbors would follow suit one after the other. Nor did this seem, at the time, an idle concern. Even discounting the Sino-Soviet influence, the "masses" really did appear to be tending toward communism. Castro had less than eighty followers when he landed in eastern Cuba in 1956. But he gained the almost unanimous support of the Cuban peasantry, and decisively overthrew the Batista regime within three years. Ernesto "Che" Guevara, an Argentinian who had joined Castro's rebellion, was convinced that all of South America was ripe for revolution. Confident that he could duplicate the campaign in Cuba, Guevara went on to Bolivia at the head of a small but resolute band of guerrillas. Captured and executed by the Bolivian army in 1967, Guevara became a heroic symbol of revolt to radical sympathizers all over the world.

FIDEL CASTRO ADDRESSES A CROWD IN CAMAGÜEY, CUBA SHORTLY AFTER HIS OVERTHROW OF THE BATISTA REGIME IN JANUARY 1959. CASTRO'S ALLIANCE WITH SOVIET RUSSIA GAVE THE LATTER A CRUCIAL FOOTHOLD IN THE WESTERN HEMISPHERE, MAKING CUBA A FOCAL POINT OF THE COLD WAR.

The Central Intelligence Agency plan to destabilize the Castro regime became a top priority once Kennedy took office. Though in fact Castro had resisted any direct Soviet manipulation, Kennedy regarded him as little more than a stooge of the communist conspiracy, whose elimination was essential not only to national security but to the very prestige of the new administration. In view of the communist alliance, however, any open attack on Cuba was out of the question, as it might have been tantamount to declaring war on the Soviet Union. The covert operation that resulted from such considerations came to be known as the Bay of Pigs fiasco.

On April 15, 1961 United States B-26 bomber planes (which had been doctored to look Cuban) commenced air strikes against three military bases in Cuba. At the last moment, Kennedy, wanting to keep the plan at a "low profile," had ordered the number of "rebel" planes reduced from sixteen to six, and as a result only six out of fifty-five planes in the Cuban Air Force were destroyed. Pilots returned from their missions to Miami, claiming to be Cuban defectors. Nobody was fooled: the Cuban government identified the United States B-26s and announced that their country was "the victim of a criminal imperialist attack which violates all the norms of international law." Meanwhile, one of the "defectors" who had landed in Florida was recognized by American reporters as a member of the Cuban exile community based in Miami. This came as a shocking embarrassment to United States Ambassador Adlai Stevenson who, after repeated assurances from the Kennedy Administration, had been eloquently denying charges of United States involvement at the United Nations.

Despite these less-than-auspicious tidings, Kennedy ordered the exiles' 2506 Brigade, about 1,400 men, to proceed with their landing in Las Villas Province at the Bay of Pigs. Then, alarmed over the rising furor at the United Nations, Kennedy abruptly cancelled the second air strike that had been planned to cover the invasion force. It was still hoped, at any rate, that the supposedly vast anti-Castro underground would rise up, inspired, and join the putsch from within. This didn't pan out. Cuban militia were waiting

CASTRO WITH ARGEN-
TINEAN REVOLUTION-
ARY ERNESTO "CHE"
GUEVARA. AFTER
SERVING FOR SEV-
ERAL YEARS IN CAS-
TRO'S GOVERNMENT,
GUEVARA WENT ON
TO LEAD A COMMUN-
IST INSURRECTION
IN BOLIVIA, WHERE
HE WAS EXECUTED
IN 1967.

Anticommunist paranoia led to disastrous bungling on the part of the United States in its relations with Fidel Castro's Cuba. Despite his revolutionary mystique, Castro had not aligned himself with the orthodox Communist Party when he first came to power. Nevertheless, the United States made little attempt to come to terms with Castro; diplomatic ties were cut at the outset, and when Castro nationalized huge areas of land that had been owned by United States companies, all trade between the two countries was suspended as well. Thus Cuba was ham-handedly delivered into the welcoming arms of the Soviet Union; Castro nationalized all the main industries, many of which had been American-owned, and the Soviets proceeded with a massive aid program.

for the invaders as they landed, and Soviet-built jets promptly sank two of their ships, containing ammunition reserves and almost all communication equipment.

"This thing has turned sour in a way you wouldn't believe!" Robert Kennedy blurted to Senator George Smathers that night, as reports began to roll in from the Bay of Pigs. While the Soviets gleefully denounced the "cowardly aggression" of "American hirelings," and Castro accused the United States of wishing to return black Cubans to slavery, and Adlai Stevenson twisted slowly in the wind, Kennedy and his advisors sat pondering their next move. As Peter Collier and David Horowitz describe the scene in The Kennedys:

> Admiral Arleigh Burke said they should allow one of the destroyers in the task force lying just offshore to shell the Cuban positions to give the besieged invasion force some relief. [President Kennedy] answered sharply, 'Burke, I don't want the U.S. involved in this!' Raising his own voice, the Admiral replied: 'Hell, Mr. President, but we are involved!'...[Robert Kennedy] sat miserably off to the side, murmuring over and over, 'We've got to do something, we've got to do something.'

Manuel Artime, the civilian commander of the 2506 Brigade, remembers the disaster that followed: "We fought on the beach and in the surrounding area for three days, without rest, always waiting for the American support that never came. On the third day, with Cuban tanks in sight, we ordered a retreat. Most of those remaining headed into the swamps; a few swam away or found a boat and escaped. In the swamps many died, and the rest of us were captured."

Faced with irrefutable evidence, Kennedy was forced to publicly acknowledge full responsibility for the invasion. The concept of a "missile gap" became overshadowed by that of a "credibility gap"—that is, the disparity between the truth and the official version of events as circulated by the United States government. And a few months later, Castro formed the Cuban Communist Party and pledged a firmer commitment to his partnership with the Soviet Union.

Shortly after his inauguration, Kennedy invited Khruschev to meet at a summit in Vienna, scheduled for June. This gesture was more a matter of symbol than substance, as Khruschev, after his acrimonious departure from Paris only a few months before, was not expected to accept such an invitation. But accept he did, seeming doubly eager to proceed in the wake of the Bay of Pigs disaster. He was convinced by then that Kennedy was an indecisive young man who could be bullied, having lacked the aplomb to carry out his illicit invasion of Cuba with the same ruthless disregard for world opinion as Khruschev had shown in Hungary. For his part, Kennedy saw the summit as an opportunity to regain some of his waning credibility.

© Wide World Photos

A CUBAN SOLDIER GLOATS OVER THE WRECKAGE OF A U.S. BOMBER PLANE, SHOT DOWN DURING THE APRIL 1961 INVASION OF CUBA AT THE BAY OF PIGS—A DISASTROUS ATTEMPT BY THE KENNEDY ADMINISTRATION TO OUST CASTRO.

The issue that loomed foremost was the fate of Berlin. Since 1958, Khruschev had demanded an end to wartime treaties that ensured the presence of NATO troops in the city. In doing so, the Soviets made much of the "German threat," the possible recurrence of Nazi aggression, a bogey used in propaganda to keep Eastern Europe faithful to the alliance and to gain sympathy in the West. In reality, the Western military presence in Berlin provided incentive for some 6,000 East Germans who fled daily to the West for refuge. This became an intolerable embarrassment to the Soviets, and by 1961 they seemed prepared to go to war over the issue.

The Vienna Summit served only to make matters worse. Khruschev spent much of the first day lecturing Kennedy on Communist doctrine—and the Soviet Union's "duty" as a revolutionary nation to assist "wars of liberation," and so forth—and by the time they finally got around to the subject of Berlin, both men were peevish. Khruschev stated his position by way of an ultimatum: the Soviet Union was setting a deadline for NATO to sign a new treaty that would effectively remove all Western troops from Berlin. Kennedy, more than ever determined to stand up to Khruschev, responded that the United States would defend Berlin "at any risk." At this point, according to one source, "the meeting began to go very badly in terms of table banging and talk of missiles flying."

Back home, Kennedy addressed the nation, warning that a showdown was imminent. "I hear it said that West Berlin is militarily untenable," he said. "And so was Bastogne. And so in fact was Stalingrad. Any dangerous spot is tenable if men—brave men—will make it so." He asked for a $3-billion increase in the defense budget, a doubled draft call, and a massive civil defense program, stressing the need for public and private bomb shelters.

A thirty-one-page booklet titled The Family Fallout Shelter was therefore issued by the Office of Civil and Defense Mobilization. This provided step-by-step instructions for the building of five basic shelters, from the simple and inexpensive Basement Concrete Block to a "deluxe" unit guaranteed to house six people comfortably, complete with baffle walls, centrifugal blower, and a twelve-gauge metal door to keep mutant intruders at bay. But for those Americans who doubted their ability to construct with their own hands (as they might, for instance, a backyard barbecue pit) such shelters as would sustain the shock of a fifty-megaton H-Bomb blast (the pamphlet recommends twenty-eight inches [70 cm] of "firmly packed" gravel for this), inexpensive pre-fab units were available. But why skimp? One was, after all, going to be down there a lonnng time. Some models, priced accordingly, were veritable inverted chateaus, offering such features as wine cellars, pool tables, and trompe l'oeil windows revealing two-dimensional views of lush, pre-Apocalyptic landscapes.

The moment of truth in Berlin came on August 12 when, unexpectedly, the East Germans began constructing a brick-and-barbed-wire barrier across the city in the middle of the night. Kennedy responded the next day by sending a massive convoy of armored trucks into Berlin via the Autobahn. The world held its breath; a faint, rhythmic gravel-slapping reverberated throughout suburban America. Robert Kennedy said later: "The president felt strongly, as I did, that we were close to war at that time."

As it turned out, though, the Wall ended the crisis: with her citizens safely trapped, East Germany was less concerned about NATO troops in West Berlin, while the United States, albeit under protest, allowed the Wall to stand. And presently the Soviet treaty deadline was withdrawn.

The Bay of Pigs fiasco had but briefly discouraged the Kennedy administration in its effort to remove Castro. After the botched invasion, the CIA prepared a memo that concluded: "There can be no long-term living with Castro as a neighbor." A special task force (code-named "Mongoose") led by Robert Kennedy was formed to coordinate the "secret war" against Cuba, with the directive that "all efforts should be made to develop new and imaginative approaches [to] the possibility of getting rid of the Castro regime." No approach, however risky or bizarre, was barred from consideration: yet another clandestine invasion was in the works, and the CIA went on with its ingenious schemes for bringing about Castro's demise (e.g., depilatories to make his beard fall out, causing loss of machismo; contaminating his cigars with botulism, and other equally cartoonish plots).

In the summer of 1962 the Soviets began a massive military buildup in Cuba: by August, it was suspected that some 20,000 Soviet troops, 150 jets, 350 tanks, 1300 pieces of field artillery, and 700 antiaircraft guns had been sent to the island. When confronted, the Soviets denied the scope of the buildup, claiming that most of the cargo was comprised of various sorts of agricultural and economic aid. As for all those alleged Soviet "troops"—well, they were just advisors and whatnot. "We were watching entire boatloads of young Soviets arriving in Cuba wearing only two kinds of sport shirts," former CIA analyst Victor Marchetti remembers. "It smelled of an unsophisticated Soviet attempt to introduce military personnel." And how.

In September, U-2 photographs revealed what appeared to be Soviet surface-to-air, or "defensive," missile sites under construction in Cuba. Though alarmed, the Kennedy administration was loath to make public the fact that such defensive measures had been provoked by the United States government's "secret [though not to the Soviets] war" against Cuba. In a meeting on September 4, Robert Kennedy confronted Soviet Ambassador Anatoly Dobrynin about the missile sites; Dobryin admitted that defensive missiles had been deployed, but assured Kennedy that the Soviet Union had no intention of sending any "offensive" or surface-to-surface missiles into Cuba. The president then issued a formal statement, making it "unequivocally clear that the U.S. [will not] tolerate the introduction of offensive surface-to-surface missiles, or offensive weapons of any kind, into Cuba."

But the next month, U-2 flights brought back clinching evidence that Cuba was being prepared as an offensive strike base, leaving the entire country, save the northwest tip of Washington State, vulnerable to nuclear attack. The launchers were being built into a "ready" position. President Kennedy immediately put a call through to Soviet foreign minister Andrei Gromyko, and was again assured that the Soviet Union "would never become involved" in building any offersive military capacity in Cuba.

Without tipping his hand to the Soviets, Kennedy gathered his advisors on a crisis footing to determine U.S. options. The early consensus was that the U.S. should proceed with an immediate air strike to take out the missile sites. Moderates such as Adlai Stevenson balked, advising that the United States should offer instead to withdraw missiles from Turkey in exchange for the Soviets' missiles in Cuba. ("Adlai wanted a Munich," Kennedy would later say in disgust.) The president decided on a middle road: a naval blockade, or "quarantine," preventing any further shipments of offensive military equipment to Cuba.

On October 22, 1962 Kennedy addressed the nation to announce the blockade. He accused the Soviet Union of flagrant and repeated deception, and vowed to hold the Soviets solely responsible for any aggressive act initiated out of Cuba: "[It] shall be the policy of this nation to regard any nuclear missile launched from Cuba against any nation in the Western Hemisphere as an attack by the Soviet Union on the United States requiring a full retaliatory response upon the Soviet Union."

After speaking in a grim, hurried monotone, Kennedy paused toward the end of his speech and looked into the camera: "My fellow citizens, let no one doubt that this is a difficult and dangerous effort on which we have set out. No one can foresee precisely what course it will take, or what casualties will be incurred....The cost of freedom is always high, but Americans have always paid it. And one path we shall never choose, and that is the path of surrender or submission."

Victor Marchetti and his fellow analysts were holed up in the CIA war room when Kennedy announced the blockade, and were able to monitor its progress on giant wall maps. He remembers the atmosphere as "depressing": "We had concluded that we were on the brink of a war and would be incinerated as soon as those missiles reached Washington, D.C. We told our families to load up a station wagon full of necessities, and if they didn't receive a call from us at a certain time every night, they were supposed to drive north

17

PRESIDENT KENNEDY ARRIVES IN VIENNA FOR HIS JUNE 1961 SUMMIT WITH SOVIET PREMIER KHRUSCHEV. WITH TEMPERS FLARING OVER CONFLICTS IN CUBA AND BERLIN, THE MEETING WAS REPORTED TO GO "VERY BADLY IN TERMS OF TABLE BANGING AND TALK OF MISSILES FLYING."

to [shelters in] Pennsylvania.... The real scare came hours later. We were watching the progress of a group of ships that we suspected were carrying warheads. The atmosphere tensed as they sailed closer. Suddenly they slowed and then went dead in the water.... [We] deduced they were receiving instructions from Moscow. Then one turned about-face. We knew then it wasn't going to run the blockade. You could hear the sighs of relief. Another ship turned in its tracks. Kennedy had called Khruschev's bluff."

The Cuban Missile Crisis was the climactic event of the Cold War, followed by a long and sober thaw. The Soviet Union withdrew its missiles from Cuba and dismantled the bases, and the U.S. promised not to invade Cuba. Khruschev began to tone down his rhetoric, addressing East-West relations in terms of "peaceful coexistence."

In August 1963 two significant advances were made: on August 5 the United States, Soviet Union, and Great Britain signed the first treaty that prohibited further testing of

nuclear bombs in the earth's atmosphere; and three weeks later, the United States-Soviet "hot line" was installed, ensuring speedy communication in case of another crisis.

That summer, President Kennedy paid a visit to beleaguered West Berlin, where he delivered a hopeful and accurate prophecy:

> Freedom is indivisible and when one man is enslaved who are free? When all are free, then we can look forward to that day when this city will be joined as one and this country and this great continent of Europe in a peaceful globe. When that day finally comes—as it will—the people of West Berlin can take sober satisfaction in the fact that they were in the front lines....
>
> All free men, wherever they may live, are citizens of Berlin. And therefore, as a free man, I take pride in the words: *Ich bin ein Berliner.*

Vietnam

A total of 57,605 Americans died in combat during the Vietnam War. An additional 303,700 were wounded, more than half of whom were permanently disabled. It is estimated that more than 100,000 American veterans of the Vietnam War have committed suicide since their return, while almost half a million have been treated for post-traumatic stress. Nearly four million saw duty, eleven million served in the military at the time, and over twenty-seven million were threatened by the draft, many of whom rearranged their lives to avoid it. Then, of course, there were the mothers, fathers, brothers, sisters, wives, children, friends, and lovers of those who fought, died, disappeared, protested, or left the country.

And what about the Vietnamese? In South Vietnam, 220,357 were killed in action and 499,000 wounded. Combat fatalities among the North Vietnamese and Vietcong armies are probably incalculable, but are estimated as nearly 950,000, number of wounded unknown. Hundreds of thousands of Vietnamese civilians died, many in the American bombing of the North. By the time the war ended in April 1975, more than half of the South's population had become refugees.

This does not account for "neutral" Cambodia, on which the United States dropped three times as many bombs as on Japan in World War II. After Cambodia fell to the communist Khmer Rouge, a few weeks before communist take-overs in South Vietnam and Laos, millions of civilians were slaughtered as part of a genocidal "reform" program.

Those are the numbers, or some of them anyway.

The first priority of United States foreign policy after World War II was the containment of worldwide communism, to which end all means seemed justified. This usually meant supporting, if only for an interim of "stabilization," puppet regimes that were at best ineffectual, and at worst corrupt and tyrannical, as well as ineffectual. President Ngo Dinh Diem, who assumed leadership of French-controlled South

Archive Photos

Vietnam in 1954, was of the latter. Nevertheless, President Eisenhower pledged that year to assist Diem in "developing and maintaining a strong, viable state capable of resisting attempted subversion or aggression through military means," and so sent in the first few hundred United States military advisors, along with massive arms support and economic aid.

Before that, the United States had backed the French colonial administration in the Indochina War against the "Vietminh," the Communist Vietnamese nationalists who had proclaimed an independent government after Japan's defeat in World War II. In 1949 France granted token sovereignty to Vietnam, Cambodia, and Laos, declaring them "associated states" of the French Union. This failed

THE "MARCH FOR VICTORY," APRIL 1970, IN WHICH 50,000 AMERICANS PARADED THROUGH WASHINGTON, D.C. IN SUPPORT OF THE WAR. AT THIS TIME, HOWEVER, THOSE WHO STILL APPROVED OF U.S. POLICY IN VIETNAM WERE DECIDEDLY OF THE MINORITY.

1 9

to appease Communist insurgents, who went on to rout the French at Dien Bien Phu in 1954, leading to armistice negotiations that ended the war. At that time, the United States was paying for 78 percent of the French war effort.

The Geneva Agreement of 1954 temporarily divided Vietnam into northern and southern parts, with Ho Chi Minh's Communist government at Hanoi in the north and Diem's at Saigon in the south. The Agreement provided for free elections in 1956 to reunify Vietnam one way or the other; the communists, with their superior political organization and vast popular support, were fully expected to prevail. Aware then that a "free," democratic Vietnam could not be attained democratically, Diem blocked the elections, with support from the United States government. Hence Communist rebels in the south formed an insurgent guerilla force—the "Vietcong" (VC), meaning "Vietnamese Communists"—which, with mounting reinforcement from the North, commenced terrorist attacks on the Saigon government in 1957.

The strategic, and moral, dilemma for the United States, in Vietnam and elsewhere, was this: how to impose a system of government on a country that clearly violates the will of its people, who are determined to resist? Soviet Russia was able to subjugate its satellites by use of sheer, ruthless force (and geographical proximity was key to preserving the status quo), an approach that, after all, is contrary to the principles upon which the "Free World" is putatively based. But apart from ruthless force, perhaps involving the systematic annihilation of both military and civilian populations, it is all but impossible to overpower a pervasive guerilla army, particularly, as in the case of the Vietcong, one that is well armed, sheltered by the terrain, and above all, supported by the people.

This is where the "hearts and minds" thesis came in. General Edward Lansdale, who orchestrated the counter-insurgency campaign against Huk guerillas in the Philippines (and served as a model for the hero of Graham Greene's novel, The Quiet American), was dismayed by initial United States procedure in South Vietnam, noting the futility of training Diem's army to fight a conventional war against the Vietcong. In a report he prepared for the Kennedy administration, Lansdale pointed out that something more than "killing guerillas" was required. The local peasantry would have to be persuaded, "taught," that democracy was a desirable alternative. This meant standing by the people under siege, protecting their villages, and learning their language, all the while extolling the virtues of democracy. The people, Lansdale concluded, could not be beaten into submission; their "hearts and minds" had to be won.

The problem (or one problem) was that the Vietcong were "the people"—they were the ones who had fought for independence against France, while the ARVN (the South Vietnamese army) had mostly stood on the sidelines or fought for the French. Most ARVN officers were French or American trained, spoke French as a first language, and were openly and notoriously contemptuous of the peasant class. The ARVN had embraced French imperialism, and as such were not likely to win the support of the masses, much less their "hearts and minds."

David Halberstam, a Vietnam correspondent for The New York Times in 1962, remembers witnessing the failure of this policy firsthand:

> We had been sent to cover something—victory in a very small war—and it wasn't there. Even when the ARVN could muster up a few victories with the help of the new American equipment, they'd kill maybe a hundred VC. We'd hear that the VC had been wiped out of the area. Then I'd talk to an honest American who'd say, 'There's no victory at all.'
>
> 'Why? Haven't the VC been routed?'
> 'No. We've killed 1,000, and they've recruited 1,000.'
>
> And that's exactly what it was all about. I began to get a sense of what so few American generals and officials were seeing.... The Americans and their proxies had a kind of military superiority, but the VC had a total political superiority.... [The VC had] been fighting in that area, spoke a local dialect,

© Popperfoto

IN OCTOBER 1963
BUDDHIST MONKS
IN SOUTH VIETNAM
BURNED THEMSELVES
ALIVE TO PROTEST
THEIR PERSECUTION
AT THE HAND OF THE
U.S.-BACKED DIEM
REGIME.

and was one of the peasants. He understood them, understood their grievances.

By the spring of 1963, millions of peasants were being impounded by the ARVN in "strategic hamlets," their hearts and minds all the more sedulously influenced. The Diem regime, which had lost the support of many of its own people, began to rely on its American-trained secret police, led by Diem's hated brother-in-law, Ngo Dinh Nhu, to crack down on its political opponents, both Communist and non-Communist. When Buddhist monks raised ceremonial flags on the Buddha's birthday, an act that had been forbidden by the Catholic Diem, Nhu ordered his secret police to storm pagodas in Hue, killing several people. The monks began

to burn themselves alive in protest, to which Madame Nhu responded by offering to provide mustard for the "barbecues." Thus it came as no great surprise, least of all to the United States government, when Diem and Nhu were murdered in a coup on November 2, 1963.

President Kennedy, a firm believer in the "domino theory," remained publicly adamant in his support of an official American "advisory" role in Vietnam: "For us to withdraw from this effort would begin a collapse not only of South Vietnam but of Southeast Asia," he declared in a press conference. "So we are going to stay there." Privately, he was less sure. Around this time he remarked to a friend: "We've got to face the facts that the odds are about a hun-

MORE THAN 500
VETERANS GATHER
IN NEW YORK FOR
A VETERAN'S DAY
RALLY AGAINST
THE WAR.

INSET: AS ANTIWAR
PROTESTERS BURN
THEIR DRAFT CARDS
IN NEW YORK'S UNION
SQUARE, THESE IRATE
PATRIOTS HECKLE
THEM FROM ACROSS
THE STREET.

dred to one that we're going to get our asses thrown out of Vietnam."

Nowhere was the question of a so-called "credibility gap" more pertinent than in the United States government's handling of the media with regard to Vietnam. As the policy of propping up one incompetent dictator after another was proven time and again to be a grotesque failure, the United States gravitated more toward direct military involvement, deciding that if nothing could be done about the Vietcong (for the time being), at least something could be done about the press. Various congressmen and State Department officials were flown regularly to Vietnam on "fact-finding missions," for the express purpose of bringing back fabricated reports on the war's splendid progress. The generals and military press liaisons were well-oiled cogs in what Halberstam described as a "bullshit machine," programmed to maintain that all was well in the face of even the most wildly contradictory evidence.

Such was the case with the battle of Ap Bac, one of the first massive engagements of the war, and a dire indication of things to come. Though the ARVN had cornered an entire VC battalion on three sides, as usual vastly outnumbering the VC on the ground and covered from the air by swarms of American bombers and helicopters, the VC still managed to shoot down five helicopters, kill several ARVN and American personnel, then get away more or less unscathed. The ARVN reinforcements had failed to block off the VC's escape route.

"An entire ARVN armored brigade stood by," Halberstam recalls, "afraid to charge across the paddy field toward the tree line. They just wouldn't do it. They refused their [superior officers'] commands.

"The next day I ran into General Harkins at the site. 'Gentlemen,' he addressed a few reporters, 'this is a great victory. We have them in a trap, and we're just about to spring it.' The enemy was long gone and the ARVN were killing their own men by blind shelling. I'll never forget it…. 'A great victory.'"

Reporters such as Halberstam and his Times colleague Neil Sheehan, who painted a gloomy picture of the war, were vilified and harassed by United States authorities. They were denied access to the front by way of a preferential "waiting list" for press helicopters, and were forced to bribe cabdrivers to take them to the outskirts of a battle. President Kennedy made a personal call to the Times publisher, demanding that Halberstam be removed for "negative reporting." And when Halberstam received a Pulitzer Prize in 1964 for his coverage of the war, Lyndon Johnson actually denounced him as a traitor to his country.

Perhaps the pinnacle of American malfeasance was the Tonkin Gulf Resolution, which would serve as the only legal basis for the undeclared war in Vietnam. On August 4, 1964 two United States destroyers, the Maddox and the Turner Joy, patrolling off the shores of North Vietnam in the Gulf of Tonkin, reported that they had come under torpedo attack from North Vietnamese ships. That night, President Johnson announced to the nation that strikes were being carried out against North Vietnam as a result of "unprovoked attacks" on United States vessels. Prior to this announcement, a cable had arrived at the Pentagon from the captain of the Maddox: "Review of action makes many recorded contacts and torpedos fired appear doubtful. Freak weather effects and overeager sonar man may have accounted for many reports. No actual, visual sightings by Maddox. Suggest complete evaluation before any further action."

Hanoi protested that the alleged attacks on the Maddox and the Turner Joy had never taken place, and further accused the United States of violating its territorial waters and engaging in covert raids against North Vietnam. The United States denied the charges. President Johnson went before Congress to propose his Tonkin Gulf Resolution, which would authorize him to "repel any armed attack against the forces of the United States and to prevent further aggression." Secretary of Defense Robert McNamara subsequently assured a Senate panel that the attacks by the North Vietnamese in the Gulf of Tonkin had been "unequivocal and unprovoked."

Daniel Ellsberg, then a defense analyst at the Pentagon, learned the truth of the matter shortly after the resolution

A VIETNAMESE BOY
RUNS IN TERROR FROM
AN AERIAL NAPALM
ATTACK IN TRANG
BANG, SOUTH
VIETNAM.

© UPI/Popperfoto

had passed Congress: "[The] Hanoi charges had been correct, our denials false. Clandestine CIA attacks against North Vietnam, totally controlled by the United States, had preceded…the supposed North Vietnamese attack of August 4th. Moreover, I learned that our destroyers were in fact on a deliberately provocative intelligence patrol close to the shores of North Vietnam."

Five years later Ellsberg gave copies of the "Pentagon Papers," a classified government study on decision-making in Vietnam, to the Senate Foreign Relations Committee. The study established, among other things, that the Tonkin Gulf Resolution had been drafted in advance of the alleged attacks, and that the CIA raids in North Vietnam had been devised as a means of provoking such attacks and thereby justifying the resolution. As a result of these disclosures, the Tonkin Gulf Resolution was repealed in 1970. The next year, Ellsberg leaked the Pentagon Papers to various newspapers,

and was then indicted on charges of espionage, theft, and conspiracy, which carried a maximum sentence of 115 years. These charges were later dismissed when it was discovered that numerous acts of illegal misconduct had been committed against Ellsberg by the United States executive branch, including breaking into the office of Ellsberg's psychiatrist and stealing files.

The chicanery that went into the passage of the Tonkin Gulf Resolution was driven largely by desperation: by mid-1964, South Vietnam was on the brink of defeat. In the wake of Diem's murder, a string of unstable governments had come and gone, the overall fecklessness of which was reflected and surpassed by the ARVN leadership. Moreover, there was a considerable morale gap, as it were, between the ARVN and the VC: ARVN troops had to grapple with the absurdity of risking their lives in support of a series of precarious, ad hoc governments, to preserve the favored status of their class under imperialist control; the VC fought for a cause that could be stated in such lofty terms as the "Liberation of the People" and the rightful self-determination of their country. Considered in that light, it is perhaps not surprising that the ARVN were plagued with desertions while the VC flourished, forever replenishing itself with the support of an independence-minded peasantry. Toward the end of 1964, the VC were destroying ARVN units at an average rate of one battalion a week, and things were about to get worse: United States intelligence indicated that three North Vietnamese Army regiments were poised to invade South Vietnam.

From the passage of the Tonkin Gulf Resolution to the end of 1965, United States troop strength in Vietnam rose from 23,000 to over 180,000. Commanding General William C. Westmoreland committed most of the incoming troops to the Central Highlands, where the North Vietnamese invasion forces were concentrated. At the outset, the United States suffered heavy casualties at the battle of the Ia Drang Valley, which nevertheless pushed the Communists into Cambodia and saved the South from invasion. After massive U.S. reinforcements, a pattern of commitment was set: the

Marines were assigned to the northern provinces (I Corps), the Army to the central region (II Corps) and around Saigon (III Corps), and, until they were finally overwhelmed, the ARVN fought alone in the Mekong Delta (IV Corps).

By 1966, after the immediate threat of a major communist offensive had been quashed, a primary United States objective was to concentrate troops around villages and hamlets, thereby "protecting" the peasants from the insurgents (presuming, as ever, that one could be properly distinguished from the other), and, with a reformed sense of purpose, converting the peasants' hearts and minds. This "pacification" program was supported by South Vietnamese and United States civilian agencies, which provided benevolent services for the peasants while the military went about eliminating local guerillas and their infrastructure. Alas, the latter sometimes meant eliminating the peasants themselves, even the mildest of whom often proved to be zealous insurgents.

A disabled American veteran, interviewed anonymously by writer Annie Gottlieb, remembers a sadly typical episode arising from the "pacification" program:

> We [were] sitting in camp around a small fire, thirty, maybe forty yards from a small village of South Vietnamese people.... The Charlie that walked into the camp was about seven years old at the most.... I noticed he had his hands in his pockets when he came to camp. One pocket bulged a little more than the other.... He walked into the circle and stood there looking around for a minute.... I just happened to look back up. And his hand came out of his pocket with a grenade in it. ... The child dropped the grenade at his feet. It killed the child, two men, and put thirteen in the hospital.

Every effort was made to lure the guerillas away from the main population. Forays into the dense Vietnamese countryside, called "search-and-destroy" missions, were conducted by United States units in order to bring guerillas out of hiding and into battle. Such missions achieved their purpose all too often, with stranded U.S. troops being ambushed by guerillas, who were capable of striking fast and then disappearing into a complex network of tunnels and bunkers. Napalm explosives and chemical defoliants were used to expose the terrain so that guerillas could be routed out and their sanctuaries destroyed. This razed much of the forests (enough timber to meet the country's needs for thirty years), but had little actual strategic effect: in fact, it drove guerillas back to heavily populated civilian areas, which were (for the most part) exempt from the bombing. Guerillas then were able to circumvent United States "pacification" troops with the help of local civilians, with whom they hid themselves and blended. Thus the "hearts and minds" mandate became an ever riskier proposition.

Given the increasing indivisibility of civilians and guerillas, certain villages were declared "free-fire zones," which is to say part of the "front"—in a war without real front lines. This led to insupportable tension and tragic, inevitable errors. Veteran Ron Kovic, author of Born on the Fourth of July, remembers attacking

> a hut that supposedly contained a sapper team which had been planting explosives on our boats. When we ran into the hut it was covered with babies and children and men with their brains blown out—it was an unbelievable mess. My men sat down and started crying. I started to shake and puke. Villagers screamed and shouted and cursed at us. I tried to patch the bodies together.... A chopper came and picked up a boy and his foot fell off. I picked his foot up and bandaged it back on his leg and put him in the chopper.
>
> A lieutenant came up and asked how many Vietcong we'd killed. I told him we hadn't killed any.

After a while, troops took to calling the policy of "winning hearts and minds" by its suggestive acronym: WHAM. At first, the range of targets was limited to specific military installations in North Vietnam, expanding later to include suspected "enclaves" throughout the north and in remote

A U.S. SOLDIER RUNS FOR COVER IN SAIGON DURING THE "TET OFFENSIVE" OF 1968. THIS MASSIVE OFFENSIVE PROVED THE STRENGTH OF COMMUNIST FORCES IN VIETNAM, SHATTERING THE CREDIBILITY OF THE JOHNSON ADMINISTRATION, WHICH HAD INSISTED THAT "VICTORY IS IN SIGHT."

OPPOSITE PAGE: A FEW OF THE HALF-MILLION AMERICANS WHO MARCHED ON WASHINGTON FOR THE VIETNAM MORATORIUM WEEKEND IN NOVEMBER 1969.

© Popperfoto

regions of the south as well. Communist supply routes running through adjacent Laos, known as the Ho Chi Minh Trail, were also included as bombing targets, drawing Laos into the war as an increasingly important theater of conflict. The main objective of the bombing was to compel communists to negotiate a settlement of the war, which they repeatedly refused to do. Every so often, after a particularly ruinous series of bombings, President Johnson would cease the attacks in the hope that the communists had reconsidered; but Hanoi's position remained constant—there would be no negotiations without the "unconditional withdrawal" of United States and other foreign forces from Vietnam. This despite frequent assurances from Johnson's military advisors that the communists were ready to relent.

In August 1967 a congressional committee began hearings to investigate the progress of the air war in Vietnam. To the committee's surprise, Secretary of Defense Robert McNamara agreed to testify, declaring that the bombing campaign was a failure. The White House was stunned and furious. McNamara had deliberately avoided clearing his testimony with Johnson, knowing that clearance would not be granted. By then McNamara had become privately tormented by his role in furthering the war, and had despaired of Johnson, who became all the more intransigent as the situation worsened. The president seemed bent on redeeming himself in Vietnam, and would settle for nothing less than "clear-cut" victory, a goal that McNamara had finally come to perceive as futile. After his statement to the committee, McNamara was shunted off to head the World Bank. To put a good face on what otherwise was a major public-relations calamity, Johnson awarded the Medal of Freedom to McNamara, praising him as "the very best that we have." McNamara wept at the ceremony, unable to speak, looking for all to see like a broken man.

At this time public opinion was divided almost evenly between those who were for the war—and who, if anything, advocated intensified, all-out bombing—and those against it. McNamara's pessimism notwithstanding, the United States military reported that steady gains were being made, and that, far from there being a "stalemate," as so many kept insisting, the communists' collapse was imminent. General Westmoreland sent glowing telegrams to the White House: "Friendly forces have seized the military initiative from the enemy.… He has been prevented from employing his primary strategy of mounting large-scale offensives because of steadily improving friendly military strengths." Clark Clifford, McNamara's successor as Secretary of Defense, later wrote that "[such] assertions…must rank among the most erroneous assessments ever sent by field commanders."

Just before daybreak on January 30, 1968, in the midst of a seven-day truce called to celebrate the Chinese "Tet" New Year holidays, a massive communist offensive began in the northern and central provinces of South Vietnam, spreading by nightfall to Saigon and the Mekong Delta. The American embassy in Saigon came under heavy mortar attack and the grounds of the Presidential Palace were overrun. Within days, some 84,000 communist troops had attacked five out of six major cities in South Vietnam, thirty-nine of forty-four provincial capitals, and at least seventy-one of 245 district towns. Fighting around Saigon and Hue went on for several weeks, resulting in a million new refugees and thousands of civilian casualties. Communists controlled Hue for over a month, executing more than 3,000 civilians. By the time the first wave of attacks had subsided, more than 4,000 American troops had been killed, nearly 5,000 South Vietnamese, and as many as 58,000 communists, the latter consisting mostly of irregular units, local militia, and farmers who had been forced into suicide missions. The communists suffered relatively minor losses to their main forces and regular units, most of whom were kept on the sidelines during the most devastating intervals of the attack.

Clark Clifford wrote that the Tet offensive "made a mockery of what the American military had told the public about the war, and devastated Administration credibility." A further casualty of Tet was the United States "pacification" program: "Those in charge of the program had predicted that 1968 would be the year of decisive success," Clifford wrote. "Tet shattered more than this empty rhetoric: with the towns and cities of South Vietnam under attack, most of the villages and hamlets were undefended, and the Vietcong forces were able to deal the pacification program a serious blow."

President Johnson tried to downplay Tet, declaring the communist effort "a dismal failure"—this on February 2, three days into the offensive. Senator George Aiken of Vermont, responding on behalf of senate Republicans, said acidly: "If this is failure, I hope the Vietcong never have a major success." The American public turned angrily against the war, its sense of outrage quickened by a growing awareness of ongoing, high-level deception over the war's progress. Even Walter Cronkite, in his role as mild, avuncular

AMERICAN SOLDIERS
STAND AROUND A
TAPED-OFF CLEARING
IN THE VIETNAMESE
VILLAGE OF MY LAI,
INVESTIGATING THE
ALLEGED MASSACRE
OF 109 CIVILIANS
THERE.

arbiter of the public mood, took it upon himself to condemn the war on national television.

General Westmoreland professed only mild dismay, dismissing any prospect of a negotiated ceasefire as "unacceptable": "We would just like the North Vietnamese to go home and turn in their weapons," he quipped, a few weeks into the offensive. Meanwhile, he requested reinforcements: 206,000 troops, to be sent incrementally over the coming year, augmenting the nearly 540,000 United States servicemen already in Vietnam. This was the last straw. On March 31, 1968 President Johnson called for a partial halt of the bombing, announcing that direct talks between the United States and North Vietnam would begin in Paris in May. He also announced that he would not seek reelection for another term.

Though the Paris negotiations made little progress toward a settlement of the war, President Nixon—who had campaigned on the promise to achieve "peace with honor"

in Vietnam—took steps to end the United States ground combat role. In July 1969 he unveiled his "Nixon Doctrine," which disavowed any future American combat commitment in foreign ground wars between rival political factions. On the basis of this, Nixon initiated his program of "Vietnam-ization," the gradual withdrawal of United States ground forces from Vietnam, preceded by a massive buildup of ARVN forces, so that South Vietnam could assume sole responsibility for its ground defense. The president announced the withdrawal of 25,000 American troops in July, and 85,000 more in October. With "Vietnamization" well under way, the United States began its secret bombing campaign against long-inviolable communist bases in Cambodia.

At that time, especially, the American public was primed to take a very dim view of expansion into Cambodia. (One consequence of its eventual disclosure in April 1970 was the demonstration at Kent State.) Antiwar sentiment was at its peak, as witnessed by the Vietnam Moratorium weekend in November 1969, when over half a million citizens had marched on Washington to demand an end to the war (though Nixon confessed afterward that he'd been watching football on television, and had missed the whole thing). With the collapse of the United States "pacification" program after the Tet offensive, rumors of United States atrocities in Vietnam abounded; one of the placards at the Moratorium march, REMEMBER THE PINKVILLE 109, referred to one such incident, not yet familiar to most Americans, which would come to be known as the "My Lai Massacre."

The operation at My Lai had begun as a search-and-destroy mission in an area where there were reportedly hundreds of Vietcong. Instead, American soldiers found what appeared to be women and children and old men.

"It was a Nazi-type thing," said Michael Terry, a Mormon GI who had witnessed the killings. "[They] just shoved the Vietnamese into ditches and killed them."

The young man who had ordered the cold-blooded slaughter of 109 Vietnamese civilians was Lieutenant William L. Calley, Jr., described by Seymour Hersch, the reporter who broke the story, as "a meek, mild-mannered agricultural-school-graduate type of guy."

"All my sources agreed that I should find Paul Meadlo," Hersch recalls, "[the soldier who] had done most of the shooting. There were rumors that he had been very upset about it. GIs saw him as a big, dumb farm kid, one of the few Calley could push around."

Meadlo, whose foot had been blown off by a land mine the day after My Lai, was living with his parents and pregnant wife at the family farm in Indiana. Hersch contacted Meadlo's mother, who, after some hesitation, agreed to let him interview her son. "I gave them a good boy," she remarked, "and they made him a murderer."

With his mother and wife present, Meadlo told Hersch about the incident in (Hersch recalled) "a straight, calm, unaffected voice…very flat and nasal":

> "We were choppered into the landing zone
> and got out," Meadlo said, "expecting it to be
> hot; filled with the enemy. Nobody was there.
> We started moving in. Somebody saw an old
> man by a well and shot him. Calley came up
> to me at one point and said, 'Round every-
> body up.' I rounded 'em up and he said, 'Take
> care of 'em.' So I watched them, and when he
> came back, he said, 'Hey, Meadlo, I said take
> care of 'em.' So then I just started shooting.
> … Later we had a bunch more, and Calley
> told me to push them in a ditch, and he
> named two or three other guys, and then
> we just shot them in the ditch."

At his court-martial in 1971, Calley testified that he had been following orders. He was found guilty of premeditated murder.

By the end of 1971, the "Vietnamization" of the war was almost complete, with the United States military presence reduced to 184,000 from a peak of 543,400 in April 1969. The bombing of Cambodia and North Vietnam continued. In March 1972, the United States broke off the Paris peace talks, citing a lack of sincere cooperation on the part of the communists, and President Nixon ordered the mining of Haiphong and other North Vietnamese harbors. Talks resumed in July and were again suspended in December, followed by a massive eleven-day bombing campaign by the United States, which effected a renewed spirit of cooperation in the communists. "Peace with honor" was thus achieved a few weeks later, on January 27, 1973, when the United States and North Vietnam signed a cease-fire agreement providing for the full withdrawal of United States forces from South Vietnam, whose days of sovereignty were thence numbered. The Communists, in their turn, submitted to the release of all American prisoners of war.

In the year after the United States' withdrawal, more than 50,000 Vietnamese died in combat. In January 1975, the communists invaded Phuoc Long province and began occupation of the Central Highlands in South Vietnam. From there they moved with little resistance toward Saigon, which fell on April 30, 1975 becoming Ho Chi Minh City.

The 22nd of November

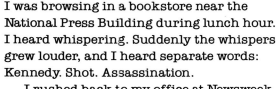

Mrs. Kennedy is deeply appreciative of your sympathy and grateful for your thoughtfulness

I was browsing in a bookstore near the National Press Building during lunch hour. I heard whispering. Suddenly the whispers grew louder, and I heard separate words: Kennedy. Shot. Assassination.

I rushed back to my office at Newsweek. Everyone was grouped around the ticker. It didn't seem possible that such a hopeful man had been killed. I got into a terrible fight with a friend who kept saying to me, 'He's going to die. Going to die.' I knew he was going to die, but I got so angry at this guy telling me. And then of course he did die....

I was an usher in the church for the funeral.... I stood and watched everyone enter, then: President Lyndon Johnson. The line stopped. I remember just looking at him.... That's when I cried. He looked so mournful, what we later came to recognize as his 'shame' expression....

It was the beginning of a long lousy slide. A certain letdown came over me.... I was jolted into realizing that maybe we didn't have any answers, maybe we didn't have the system. Kennedy had never been a revolutionary, in any sense of the word. Bobby was much more of a gut liberal than Jack. But life was never the same after Kennedy was assassinated. That's for goddamn sure.

—Benjamin C. Bradlee

In the United States House of Representatives, debate was interrupted as the news was passed to Speaker John McCormack.

"My God! My God!" he exclaimed. "What are we coming to?"

It was perhaps the single most shocking event in the nation's history—more so than any declaration of war (which tends to provoke a not unpleasant sense of exhilaration); more so than the deaths of other American presidents, due in part to television, which reported the tragedy minute by minute as it unfolded, then played and replayed the images throughout the long, dismal weekend: shots fired at the president's motorcade in Dallas…the president hit…the president dead…the alleged assassin, Lee Harvey Oswald, apprehended…Johnson sworn in on the presidential jet two hours later, with a dazed and disheveled Jackie Kennedy standing by, her pink wool suit spattered with her husband's blood…Oswald himself murdered two days later, for all to see…the funeral at Arlington…John-John saluting his father's hearse….

Handsome, witty, vigorous, John F. Kennedy seemed to personify all the best qualities of a troubled but still idealistic era: politically moderate, he was yet inclined toward such activist policies as desegregation, an expanded welfare commitment, equal pay for equal work, and such volunteer programs as the Peace Corps. He had grown in office, stumbling badly with the Bay of Pigs invasion, but redeeming himself later with his decisive handling of the Cuban missile crisis, which had enabled the Soviets to give in without being humiliated. A thaw in the cold war had followed: a few months before Kennedy's death, the nuclear test-ban treaty was signed and the United States-Soviet "hot line" installed. What he might have done in Vietnam is anybody's guess (though one doubts he would have botched it on the same sort of pathological scale as LBJ).

And then there was Kennedy's personal saga: the son of a famous and controversial father; a decorated hero of World War II; and the putative author of a Pulitzer Prize-winning book, Profiles in Courage. On his way to becoming the youngest elected president, and the first Catholic, he had overcome life-threatening Addison's disease and a crippling back ailment.

He deliberately cultivated an "heroic" public posture, although recent disclosures have tarnished that image. Nevertheless, many Americans remember with respect the high-minded speeches and all that Kennedy "stood for," and beyond that, the man himself: the sudden charming smile, piercing a moment of high gravity. That was Kennedy's "special grace," as Bradlee put it, a certain human quality which, for many, made the loss of him so heart-breaking.

PRESIDENT KENNEDY THROWS OUT THE FIRST BALL OF THE 1961 BASEBALL SEASON AT GRIFFITH STADIUM IN WASHINGTON, D.C.

DESPITE HEAVY SNOW-
FALL, THIS GROUP OF
CHINESE RED GUARDS
BEAMS HAPPILY
UNDER THE WARMING
"SUNSHINE OF GREAT
LEADER MAO'S
THOUGHT."

WORLD CONFLICT

The Chinese Cultural Revolution

Be you hippie, yippie, mod, or a member of Mao's Red Guard, the Sixties were a swell time to be young and revolutionary. In China, adolescent students and peasants, who had never known even the faintest hint of liberty, were suddenly free to roam all over the country at the government's expense, purging "revisionist" Communist Party members as well as "officeholders following the capitalist road" in schools, factories, cultural organizations, and hospitals. Thus hapless "counterrevolutionaries" were paraded about in dunce caps, flogged in cadence with some of the more spirited communist anthems, and often tortured until they either died or confessed to lurid, imaginary crimes against the regime. And the beauty of it, for those "little Red generals" who basked in the "sunshine of great leader Mao's thought," was that their victims, however randomly or unjustly persecuted, were forbidden to resist!

"You are the successors to the present revisionism-poisoned Communist regime," Mao Tse-tung told Chinese high school and university students in August 1966, having closed all schools from kindergarten up. "Destroy it and we will build a new China nearer to your heart's desire."

Mao had resigned the chairmanship of the republic in 1959 but continued as chairman of the party politburo. He had watched with growing dismay as his own brand of communism was superseded by the decadent, Soviet-style communism practiced by his successor, President Liu Shao-chi. The latter approach to communism, Mao claimed, took power away from the people and put it into the hands of a few "elitist" government officials. Under Mao's system, ideally, the people governed themselves—the country was divided into self-sufficient communes that collectively arranged for the education of their members as well as their own subsistence, deciding what goods should be produced and marketed. Most ideally—for those in power—was that any opposition to great leader Mao's system or, for that matter, anything resembling free speech or frank discussion was strictly forbidden.

Mao, whose influence had been on the wane, was faced with a dilemma in choosing the proper weapon for his putsch: he could not call on the army to remove "power holders" from office, as that would contradict a vital Maoist principle, namely, that "politics must control the gun," not vice versa; he could not rely on party or government organizations, as they were the chief targets of his purge; and he could not call on the workers, as trade unions were controlled by the party and were, besides, largely under the influence of the man whom Mao had cast as the foremost rascal of revisionism, Liu Shao-chi. Hence Mao and a few of his top henchmen, with the support of the press, turned to the most disenfranchised element of Chinese society—students and peasants in their teens and early twenties—proclaiming them all-powerful "Red Guards," whose sacred duty was to "spearhead" Mao's Great Proletarian Cultural Revolution. Their reward for an enthusiastic response to this new duty would be a chance to inherit the power of "many people in authority."

The young Red Guards executed their mission with the sort of idealistic sadism peculiar to those who have spent their lives in a state of absolute repression, and suddenly find themselves free to indulge their basest desires. With little guidance or control from the authorities, who were understandably reluctant to call attention to themselves, the Red Guards toppled a wide range of "officeholders," from military leaders to schoolteachers, many of whom had devotedly served Mao and the Communist Party long before their tormentors were born. Li Ta, a respected university president who, with Mao, was the only surviving founder of the Chinese Communist Party, was imprisoned and tortured

by Red Guards, and finally died after being deprived of crucial medicines and care. President Liu Shao-chi was ousted, though not before his wife had been lured from her home in the sacrosanct Forbidden City—tricked into thinking that one of her children had been injured—and then brutally interrogated by Red Guards, who tried to force her into confessing, on behalf of her husband and relatives, to a concoction of heinous, counterrevolutionary crimes.

The Red Guards began to factionalize at a great rate, with as many as twenty separate associations in a single school or factory. Each group boasted that it alone was orthodox in its Maoism, adopting such insistent names as "The August First Field Army Swearing to Defend the Thought of Mao Tse-tung to the Death," and attempted to discredit other Red Guard groups with a flurry of poster-pasting and pamphlet-passing and public meetings full of dueling loudspeakers. The next phase, of course, was gang warfare on a chaotic scale: in August 1968 a group of Red Guardsmen stormed an armory in Canton, appropriating some 30,000 rounds of ammunition and several hand grenades with which to assault rival headquarters in the General Trade Union Building. An admonitory telegram from Premier Chou En-lai was disregarded, and five days later the same group attacked the Canton waterworks and a power plant.

Mao had anticipated a certain amount of internecine strife among his "little Red generals," and with a sort of grandfatherly indulgence had allowed it to proceed unchecked. Once his own god-like power was restored, however, Mao abruptly stepped in and announced that all Red Guard factions were to be "discarded and disbanded."

And did these devoted young Maoists, after all that, receive their promised bequest of a "new China nearer to [their] hearts' desire?" Did they then become the "people in authority"? In a word, no. In three words, of course not. In fact, their lives became more restricted than ever, as they were ordered back to the farms, millions of them at once, to wield hoes and push plows in the glaring sunshine of great leader Mao's thought.

WORLD CONFLICT

The Six Day War

Ever since 1948, when the Jewish state was founded in Palestine, and millions of Palestinians were uprooted to refugee camps, Arab anger and frustration has mounted. Every time the Arabs have attempted to wipe Israel off the map—a tiny country, after all—they have ended up getting stomped. They tried in 1948, and again in 1956, and then, the crowning blunder, were all set to do it again in 1967, when "beleaguered" Israel dealt them a stunning sucker punch and then acquired thousands of miles of new territory.

The crisis that evolved into the "Six Day War" of 1967 began a few years earlier, as Jewish settlements near the Golan Heights came under attack from Palestinian guerillas out of Syria. As it was Israel's policy to strike back not only at guerillas but at their "host" countries too, Israeli reprisals took the form of intermittent raids against Palestinian camps and a general quid-pro-quo shelling of Syria.

In November 1966, President Nasser of Egypt responded to such "Israeli aggression" by pledging his country's support to Syria in the event of an Israeli invasion. Heartened, the Syrians complemented guerilla attacks by stepping up their own bombardment of Israeli villages from bases in the Golan Heights. Israel responded by massing troops in the demilitarized zone near the Syrian border, whereupon Nasser, fearing yet further aggression, demanded the withdrawal of United Nations emergency troops from the Israel-Egypt border, then closed the Straits of Tiran to Israeli vessels, a move that Israel had warned would mean war. Then, on May 30, 1967, Nasser signed a mutual defense pact with his long-time enemy, King Hussein of Jordan; and Israeli Defense Minister Moshe Dayan decided that, for Israel's part, the best defense was a good offense.

Before dawn on June 5, 1967, a swarm of Israeli planes flew under Egyptian radar and bombed Egypt's airfields, catching on the ground and annihilating, in one fast and very

fell swoop, the Arab world's most effective military unit, the Egyptian Air Force. Egypt hardly had a moment to muse over the rubble before Israeli tanks began pouring into the Sinai desert, smashing the Egyptian army. Nor did Israel settle for simple retreat: as the Soviet-built Egyptian tanks trundled hastily for the border, Israeli tanks (built for speed by the United States) raced around and cut them off at Mitla Pass. There they pounded and starved the Egyptians into surrender. When it was over, the Sinai was littered with the charred wreckage of practically the entire Egyptian tank fleet.

The Israelis meanwhile approached King Hussein of Jordan, asking him whether he'd like to reconsider his pact with Egypt. Hussein faithfully declined, and was thence beaten out of the entire West Bank of the River Jordan, including the "old city" portion of Jerusalem. That left Syria to reckon with, a matter of special relish to the Israelis. In the last twenty-four hours of the war, they routed the Syrians out of the Golan Heights, from which Syria had been shelling their settlements since 1948.

By the time the United Nations Security Council effected a cease-fire on June 11, Israel was sitting on the whole of Sinai, the Golan Heights, and the West Bank. They annexed Jerusalem and declared it a united city under Israeli rule. Besides huge expanses of territory, the Arab states had lost much of their productive capability, military hardware, and inestimable revenues. Israel offered to return some of the territory, in exchange for which the Arabs would have to agree to a lasting peace, that is, recognize Israel's right to exist.

The Arabs refused, partly due to pressure from the Palestine guerilla movement, whose militant faction (which opposed all compromise with Israel) had become dominant as a result of the war; partly to show, for what it was worth, that they still had their pride.

So Israel consolidated her new territories and the cycle of raids, counter-raids, and negotiations resumed, with no end in sight as the decade drew to a close.

A SOVIET TANK BURNS
IN PRAGUE DURING
THE FIRST HOURS OF
OCCUPATION.

The Invasion of Czechoslovakia

During the Fifties and the Sixties, life in the Soviet bloc just kept on getting better—mass spy trials went more or less out of vogue, and the bloody purges that had flourished under Stalin were an almost forgotten part of the perennially emended past. In this best of all possible worlds, hardline Communists thought it awfully bad form for the masses to quibble over matters like censorship, lack of personal freedom, and the numbskull party bureaucracy that frustrated every attempt to revive a generally moribund economy.

Among the satellite states, Czechoslovakia was especially close to total collapse, and in January 1968 a progressive faction of the Czech Communist party decided to take matters into its own hands. Antonin Novotny, a dusty product of Soviet taxidermy, was replaced as first secretary by the liberal-minded Alexander Dubcek, who initiated a program of reforms that, within three months, transformed Czech society. Under Dubcek, the Czechs distanced themselves from Moscow and lifted government control from the press, giving rise to a flood of invective over past abuses. And Czech citizens, free at last to travel abroad and get a better idea of just how bad they'd had it, allied behind Dubcek and spoke out as one against the Soviets.

The Soviets were a little shocked, a little hurt, and a little fearful that the contagion of liberalization would lead to the gradual rot of the entire communist system. They advised Dubcek to rein in his programs. Dubcek assured the Soviet Union that Czechoslovakia would stay faithful to the Warsaw Pact and remain communist; meanwhile he took steps to decentralize the economy and introduce a limited profit incentive, while broadening his social reforms. The "Czech experiment" was applauded throughout the West, infur-

iating the Soviets, who denounced Dubcek's initiatives as "reckless" and "disruptive." The Soviets then began to hint at direct military intervention, announcing that maneuvers were under way near the Czech border. Dubcek vowed in a radio address that liberalization would continue, and that Czech sovereignty was not threatened. President Tito of Yugoslavia came to Prague and proclaimed his support for Czech independence, an overture calculated to draw Czechoslavakia into the Tito-dominated sphere of nonaligned countries.

On August 21, 1968, under the commodious cloak of darkness, thousands of tanks manned by some half-million troops of the Warsaw Pact armies rolled over the borders and occupied Czechoslovakia. They had come, the Soviets explained, at the invitation of the Czech government, which had "requested assistance" to put down a vile, counter-revolutionary plot hatched, of course, by the shadowy forces of "Western imperialism." Dubcek, a dupe, was arrested.

Worldwide reaction was overwhelmingly negative—even a majority of non-Soviet communists were affronted. The Soviets tried to allay criticism with a sweetly reasoned essay in *Pravda* on the "necessity" of protecting socialist countries from "outside attacks." The Czech National Assembly put a hot round of shot into this canard by declaring the invasion illegal and demanding that troops be withdrawn immediately. Czech citizens united against the Soviets with nationwide nonviolent protests. Moscow, somewhat taken aback, kindly allowed Dubcek and his associates to resume their offices and, by October 1968, withdrew most of the occupying troops.

But the Czech experiment was, in fact, all over. The Soviets slyly bided their time, waited for international attention to flag, and then swiftly abolished all reforms, capping their triumph by re-booting Dubcek in April 1969.

COLONEL JOHN GLENN, JR., STANDS BESIDE HIS CAPSULE, *FRIENDSHIP 7,* IN WHICH HE BECAME THE FIRST AMERICAN TO BE LAUNCHED INTO ORBIT.

Courtesy NASA

The Space Race

Until the day when, say, a colony is founded on Jupiter (and then perhaps rival colonies, until a term like "Jovia-political" enters the vernacular), or the first palm tree is planted on a space station—until the next truly awe-inspiring break-through, it is safe to say that, where space travel is concerned, the thrill is gone. The luster of novelty has worn off. Never again, no matter what breakthroughs may come, can we expect to witness the spectacle of 9,000 Americans jammed into Grand Central Station before a gigantic television screen, all of them stricken with anxiety over the

Courtesy NASA

fate of rock-jawed, crew-cutted Colonel John Glenn, Jr., the first American in orbit (February 21, 1962), whose capsule might have disintegrated, for all anyone knew, as it rammed back into the atmosphere. It didn't, and Americans started breathing again. "Millions of working hours were lost during the day," The New York Times reported, "but no one could have begrudged this."

But, oh, how every patriotic American's blood boiled at the Russians' smugly rhyming announcement (ten months before Glenn) that "[they had] won the race/to put a man in space." Sheepishly came White House press secretary Pierre Salinger to greet reporters on that grim day, admitting that, yes, "American tracking stations have confirmed the fact that the Soviet Union has launched a satellite…"

America had been taking it on the chin in the so-called "space race" since 1957, when the Soviets' 184-pound (83 kg) *Sputnik* (meaning "fellow traveler") became the first satellite launched into orbit. In 1959 another Soviet satellite, *Luna 3,* photographed the hidden side of the moon, and the demoralized United States responded with the rather blustery announcement that "Project Mercury" was under way—a manned space program.

It was not just a matter of vain competitiveness between the superpowers (though it was mostly that): at the height of the Cold War, the prospect of one side enjoying a distinct technological advantage over the other was, to put it mildly, disconcerting. Hence it was painful indeed when, "Project Mercury" withal, the Soviets launched handsome young cosmonaut Yuri Gagarin into orbit, in the sputnik *Vostok,* meaning "East," which must have evoked in the minds of some Americans a kind of college football showdown, complete with cheerleaders: "We have won the race/To put a man in space/And with a cosmos view/We will bury you!"

"All right, then, to hell with 'Project Mercury,'" one imagines a tortured (post-*Vostok,* post-Vienna) President Kennedy saying, in effect, "so we *won't* be the first to launch a satellite, or put a man into orbit…" Instead, the United States announced yet another program, "Project Apollo," aimed at putting a man on the moon by no later than 1970. Thus the gauntlet, at a cost of twenty-five billion American 1961 dollars, was flung.

Within a year, the United States had launched its first man into space (Alan Shepard), a man into orbit (Glenn, who orbited *three* times, by the way, putting him two up on

JULY 20, 1969. ASTRO-NAUT NEIL ARM-STRONG PLANTS THE AMERICAN FLAG ON THE LUNAR SURFACE—A PHOTO OPPORTUNITY MADE POSSIBLE BY YEARS OF FRENZIED COMPETITION WITH THE SOVIETS AND MANY BILLIONS OF DOLLARS.

Courtesy NASA

Gagarin), and then, after Glenn, a couple more orbiters for good measure (Carpenter, Schirra). That same year, 1962, the U.S. launched an elaborate communications satellite, *Telstar* (which occasioned a popular tune of the same name, by ace surfer band The Ventures) as well as a Venus probe, *Mariner 2.* In 1963 the Soviet Union scored a symbolic, if not technological, victory by sending the first female cosmonaut into space, Valentina Tereshkova—a challenge that, interestingly enough, the United States chose not to answer.

For most of the Sixties, the "space race" followed a pattern: the Soviets would do something first, whereupon the Americans, a few exasperating months later, would compensate by doing the same thing better (or, rather, by doing more of the same thing). A Soviet cosmonaut took the first "space walk" in 1965, stepping out of the *Voskhod II* to float in space for ten minutes; later that year, United States astronaut Edward White "walked" around *Gemini 4* for a total of four hours and twenty-one minutes, attending to some obscure "outside repair" (meanwhile gloating, perhaps, over his peculiar niche in the *Guinness Book*). In 1966, the unmanned Soviet *Luna 9* made the first "soft" landing on the moon, transmitting pictures that proved that the surface was firm enough to land on; close behind was the U.S. *Surveyor 1,* which transmitted pictures (11,000 of them!) proving exactly the same thing. Tragedy struck both sides, but the Soviets first, in 1967: cosmonaut Vladimir Komarov was killed during the reentry of *Soyuz 1,* and United States astronauts Virgil Grissom, Edward White, and Roger Chaffee died when their spacecraft exploded on the launching pad.

Then, in 1968, the United States began at last to pull ahead, as the unmanned *Surveyor 7* made the first successful "hard" landing on the moon. And with that, the Soviets seemed to lose heart, spacewise: the expense was abominable and, really, there were other things to worry about. As a sort of final, wan little stunt, two Soviet satellites managed to "find" each other by radar while in the earth's orbit. Small potatoes! By 1968, the only real game left was putting a man on the moon—the Soviets knew it and were having none of it. By the end of the year, then, the "space race" was

Courtesy NASA

considered over (at which time, as if to punctuate the matter, albeit with grisly irony, Yuri Gagarin crashed in his plane).

And all the while the United States was getting nearer. Shortly after the *Surveyor* landing, *Apollo 8* orbited the moon with three astronauts aboard. Early the next year, *Apollo 10* brought a lunar module within 9.4 miles (15 km) of the moon's surface. Back home, the three men chosen for the historical *Apollo 11* mission—Neil Armstrong, Mike Collins, and Edwin "Buzz" Aldrin—were practicing the moonwalk in a fifty-by-fifty-foot (15-x-15-m) litterbox, plodding about with heavy equipment on their backs, a constellation of flashbulbs bursting around them.

And finally, at exactly 4:17:40 P.M. Eastern Standard Time on July 20, 1969—after the vast expense, the mighty effort, and because of the unquenchable drive to be Number One —hundreds of millions of viewers around the world saw it live: Neil Armstrong pouncing upon the powdery lunar soil.

"That's one small step for man, one giant leap for mankind."

("Having gotten here sooner/We are kings of things lunar.")

While they were there, Armstrong and Aldrin installed a "passive seismometer" to gauge quake movements on earth, as well as a hundred prismatic reflectors to help measure continental drift. They left a patriotic patch in honor of Grissom, White, and Chaffee, medals for Komarov and Gagarin, and a disk with recorded messages from seventy-two heads of state (in anticipation of what, exactly? —A polyglot ETI with a hi-fi?). They planted the flag, saluted, and seemed to frolic a bit, as Mike Collins drifted placidly overhead in the orbiting command-module.

"Why drag in such irrelevant matters as wasted dollars and power politics?" wondered Russian-American writer Vladimir Nabokov. "That gentle little minuet that despite their awkward suits the two men danced with such grace to the tune of lunar gravity was a lovely sight…. [The] strange sensual exhilaration of palpating those precious pebbles, of seeing our marbled globe in the black sky, of feeling along one's spine the shiver and wonder of it all."

OPPOSITE PAGE: ASTRO-NAUT EDWIN "BUZZ" ALDRIN HOPS OFF THE LUNAR MODULE TO BECOME THE SECOND MAN ON THE MOON.

LEFT: THE *APOLLO 11* ROCKET STANDS READY FOR LAUNCHING AT CAPE CANAVERAL.

CHAPTER TWO
PROTEST

MARTIN LUTHER KING,
JR. (1929–1968)

The Civil Rights Movement

The fundamental changes in American society that came out of the Sixties are largely products of the civil rights movement. By compelling a supposedly free nation to live up to its most basic creed—"We hold these truths to be self-evident, that all men are created equal"—civil rights activists not only furthered the cause of black men and women, but of all people disenfranchised by a predominately white, patriarchial society, whether they be Native Americans, Latin Americans, Asian Americans, women, the poor, the old, or the young. Inspired by the blacks' struggle, all would rise up and demand equal treatment by the end of the decade and beyond.

© FPG International

But to reflect on the history of the civil rights movement is in many ways as disheartening as it is inspirational. As Martin Luther King wrote: "History is the long and tragic story of the fact that privileged groups seldom give up their privileges voluntarily." For Americans, the dismal truth of that statement became sadly apparent in the Sixties, when matters were brought to a crisis.

True integration in the United States began, in principle, with the case of Brown versus Board of Education of Topeka in 1954, when the Supreme Court ruled that segregation by color in public schools was a violation of the Fourteenth Amendment. But the first significant milestone of the civil rights movement in terms of direct-action protest was the Montgomery, Alabama Bus Boycott of 1955–56.

After Rosa Parks, an elderly black woman, was arrested for refusing to give up her seat to a white man, a citywide black boycott of the segregated bus system was mobilized by Reverend Dr. Martin Luther King, Jr., then an obscure twenty-seven-year-old Baptist minister. Though white citizens hardly took the strikers seriously at first, jeering them as they made their way by carpool or on foot, the boycott turned out to be an almost unqualified success, lasting 381 days and nearly bankrupting the bus line. The mood among Montgomery whites turned anxious and hostile during the siege, and at one point King's home was bombed. Enraged blacks were on the verge of rioting, but King persuaded them to remain nonviolently committed to the boycott. When at last the United States Supreme Court declared that Alabama bus segregation laws were unconstitutional, King became world famous as a champion of Gandhi's philosophy of passive resistance.

King formed the Southern Christian Leadership Conference (SCLC) in 1957 as an organization devoted to peaceful protest throughout the South. Over the next eleven years, King's nonviolent activism would result in his being repeatedly jailed, beaten, and on one occasion stabbed; his home would be bombed twice more, and in 1964 he would become the youngest recipient ever of the Nobel Peace Prize. Such were the glories to be reaped on the road to martyrdom.

The civil rights movement of the Sixties began rather modestly, with sit-in demonstrations at lunch counters and other segregated public facilities. A nationwide boycott of Woolworth stores began on February 2, 1960 after an incident in Greensboro, North Carolina, where a group of black college students vowed to sit at a Woolworth lunch counter in shifts until they were served. "They can just sit there," the store manager said. "It's nothing to me."

Within two weeks the sit-in protests had spread to fifteen cities in five states, and a month later as many as 350 protesters were arrested in Orangeburg, South Carolina. Occasionally there was violence, often directed at white protesters, whose "nigger-loving" temerity enraged segregationists. By October 1960, four national chain stores had announced integration of counters in 112 southern cities, an important gain for the movement.

Dr. King was arrested at a sit-in demonstration in Atlanta on October 26, and initially given a twelve-month suspended sentence on a charge of "driving without a Georgia driver's license." Seeing the opportunity to make an example of King, a DeKalb County judge revoked the suspended sentence and ordered King to serve a four-month term of hard labor instead. King was then whisked off to a state penitentiary, where his supporters feared he would be killed.

"I think the maximum sentence for Martin Luther King might do him good," remarked the governor's spokesman, Peter Zack Geer. "Might make a law-abiding citizen out of him and teach him to respect the law of Georgia."

Atlanta Mayor William B. Hartsfield was quick to note: "I have made requests of all the news agencies that in their stories they make it clear that this hearing did not take place in Atlanta, Georgia."

What followed may well have determined the outcome of the 1960 presidential election. As Peter Collier and David Horowitz describe the episode in their book, The Kennedys:

> Nixon's advisers urged him to speak out [in support of King] but he didn't. [Kennedy]

> was also publicly silent, but he called King's wife, Coretta, to offer support, and [his brother] Bobby followed with a call to the judge. King was released, and his father switched his endorsement from Nixon to Kennedy, saying he would vote for the Devil himself if he wiped the tears off his daughter-in-law's face....The Sunday before the election, pamphlets describing [the Kennedys'] support of King were distributed outside black churches all over the country. And as it worked out, the black vote was crucial in such pivotal states as Illinois and Texas.

While the Kennedy administration was avowedly sympathetic toward the civil rights movement, much of the president's attention, particularly during his first year in office, was focused on the pressing business of the cold war: Cuba, Berlin, and a Soviet-sponsored guerilla campaign in Indo-

PROTESTERS MARCH OUTSIDE A WOOLWORTH'S STORE IN ATLANTIC CITY, NEW JERSEY, TO PROTEST THE CHAIN'S SEGREGATIONIST POLICIES.

china. Though he had promised throughout the 1960 campaign to sign an order desegregating public housing, Kennedy had been in office almost two years before he got around to this "stroke of a pen." Most of the dirty work on civil rights was turned over to Robert Kennedy who, as attorney general, became the administration's enforcer and was widely despised as such by the white southern establishment.

On May 4, 1961, a group of black protesters calling themselves the "Freedom Riders" left Washington, D.C. on a mission to test desegregation in southern bus facilities; when they encountered much of the usual, often brutal, resistance from police and vigilantes, the attorney general issued a carefully worded warning during an address to the University of Georgia Law School a month later:

"The hardest problems of all in law enforcement are those involving a conflict of law and local customs.... Our position is quite clear. We are upholding the law.... In all cases, I say to you today that if the orders of the court are circumvented, the Department of Justice will act. We will not stand by and be aloof. We will move."

For the most part, though, the administration's rhetoric was remarkably conciliatory. The attorney general did not appeal to white southerners to accept racial integration on the basis of its moral rectitude so much as he seemed to maintain that the morality of the issue was moot: "I happen to believe that [integration] is right. But my belief does not matter—it is now the law. Some of you may believe [that integration is] wrong. That does not matter. It is the law. And we both respect the law." Finally, in keeping with the administration's basic priorities, the attorney general tried to persuade whites that racial equality in the United States was instrumental in setting an example of freedom to the world, and thereby stemming the tide of Communism: "From the Congo to Cuba, from South Vietnam to Algiers, in India, Brazil and Iran, men and women and children are straightening their backs and listening—to the evil promises of Communist tyranny and the honorable promises of Anglo-American liberty....When parents send their children to school this fall in [the South], peaceably and in accordance with the rule of law, barefoot Burmese and Congolese will see before their eyes Americans living by the rule of law."

It was a noble thought, but, sadly and shockingly enough, a bit before its time. As "barefoot" peoples of the Third World would soon find out, a number of white Americans were decidedly unwilling to live by the rule of the law.

In 1961 a student named James Meredith at Jackson State College (a black school) applied for admission to the University of Mississippi. When the latter replied that his application had been received too late for the winter session, Meredith asked to be considered for summer admittance, but received no further response. He then wrote accusing the university of rejecting him because of his race, to which he received a letter blandly affirming that he did not meet admission requirements.

After a year of litigation, the United States Supreme Court ordered the university to admit Meredith.

"To me," Meredith says, "it wasn't the specific aim of going to school that mattered; that was just a tactical move. The bigger thing was the struggle between those who were in power and those who were not.... My objective was to bust the legal system of white supremacy in Mississippi. The

© Wide World Photos

immediate objective was to break it at any point.... I was never involved in the civil rights movement.... I had nothing, no idealism. It was strictly a war game."

And the state of Mississippi played it as such. On the day that Meredith tried to enroll, he was confronted by thousands of screaming white students outside the registration building; inside were a group of state officials, the Board of Trustees, and Governor Ross Barnett, who had appointed himself registrar for the day so he could personally refuse entrance to Meredith.

"Governor Barnett was not all bad," Meredith says. "The effect of his attitude was to keep all the attention focused on him, so that the people of Mississippi had no obligation to do anything except wait and see what he was going to do. A previous governor, Theodore Bilbo, incited the people, made them feel that the law was in their hands. It was like, 'If you don't want a nigger to vote, then visit him in the morning, you understand?' Barnett was the opposite. He communicated the message 'I will handle this, so you don't have to do anything.'"

Barnett went on handling it. Five days after Meredith's first attempt to enroll, the governor summoned him to the Capitol in order to stage an even more public defiance of the Supreme Court's authority to enforce integration. For the benefit of the assembled mob, the national media, the

entire state legislature, and a throng of jeering white Mississippians, Barnett made a statement: "I, Ross Barnett ...acting under the police powers of this state...to preserve the peace and dignity of the State of Mississippi...denied to [Meredith]...admission to the University of Mississippi."

"It was strictly a show," Meredith recalls, "though nobody told me that.... I was the only black man present. Barnett asked, 'Who is James Meredith?' I stepped forward and played the game again."

When Meredith again attempted to enroll a week later, this time successfully, he was escorted by a cordon of federal marshals. That night, Meredith was awakened in his guarded dormitory room by the sounds of rioting. The national guard had been sent in, and the mob was yelling: "Two-Four-One-Three/We Hate Kennedy!" Scuffles broke out between guardsmen and students, and by morning twenty-eight people had been shot and two killed.

"I could never figure out whether my going to school was a point they lost, or if they were just engaging in symbolic opposition," Meredith mused. "I still don't know."

In February 1963 Kennedy proposed a comprehensive civil rights bill designed to enforce voting rights and desegregation, and to eliminate discriminatory employment practices. Ever tactful, he tried to push the bill by stressing its pragmatic aspects, underplaying the moral imperative of such legislation: "This nation can afford to achieve the goals of a full employment policy—it cannot afford to permit the potential skills and educational capacity of its citizens to be unrealized."

White southerners were, for the most part, unimpressed: the doctrine of "states' rights" remained the ultimate sanction for preserving the status quo—by force, if necessary. As civil rights laws continued to be widely flouted throughout the South, Martin Luther King decided in April 1963 to commence mass nonviolent demonstrations in arch-segregationist Birmingham, Alabama, creating a crisis that would "dramatize the Negro plight and galvanize the national conscience." The attorney general pleaded with King to postpone the Birmingham campaign, as did many

WITH HELP FROM THE U.S. SUPREME COURT, JAMES MEREDITH BECOMES THE FIRST BLACK TO GRADUATE FROM THE UNIVERSITY OF MISSISSIPPI.

"I HAVE A DREAM…" MARTIN LUTHER KING GIVES THE MOST FAMOUS SPEECH OF THE CIVIL RIGHTS MOVEMENT BEFORE 250,000 SUPPORTERS IN WASHINGTON, D.C.

white religious leaders, arguing that King's approach was "untimely" and "extreme." A few weeks later, after King and thousands of other demonstrators had been put in prison, King addressed such arguments in his famous "Letter from a Birmingham Jail":

> I must confess that over the last few years I have been gravely disappointed with the white moderate…. [I had] hoped that white moderates would reject the myth of time…. It is the strangely irrational notion that there is something in the very flow of time that will inevitably cure all ills. Actually, time is neutral. It can be used either destructively or constructively…. We will have to repent in this generation not merely for the vitriolic words and actions of the bad people but for the appalling silence of the good people. We must come to see that human progress never rolls on wheels of inevitability. It comes through the tireless efforts and persistent work of men willing to be coworkers with God, and without this hard work time itself becomes an ally of the forces of social stagnation.

© Consolidated/Archive Photos

Eventually the Birmingham demonstrations began to have the desired effect. When King and his supporters persisted in the face of imprisonment and threats, the police abandoned all restraint, using clubs, attack dogs and firehoses to "subdue" the protesters. People all over the world were outraged by reports and pictures exposing the brutal tactics of Birmingham's police chief, the infamous Bull Connor. And beyond such acts committed in the name of "law and order" there was the usual, enterprising terrorism of segregationist vigilantes: the house of King's brother was dynamited, as was the motel where King made his headquarters. The confrontation abated only when the federal government stepped in to enforce a truce that promised (but could not guarantee) desegregation in Birmingham.

Elsewhere the violence continued. On June 12, 1963, NAACP leader Medgar Evers was killed, shot in the back, outside his home in Jackson, Mississippi.

"I wanted to go to the morgue, and they tried to stop me," Charles Evers, Medgar's brother, remembers. "I wanted to cry with him when no one was around. I wanted to fix his hair. I went down and stayed with him for a long time—just the two of us. I said, 'I'm never gonna let you die in vain. I'm gonna get even with him if it's the last thing I do.'

"Racism is a sickness that eats away at a person, white or black. Right then, I really wanted to kill white folks. I meant to go out and kill them by the dozens, because one of them had shot Medgar in the back. But in the morgue that night, just me and him, something kept telling me, 'Charlie, you ain't to worry. You're not going to do anything but get yourself killed…. You're not going to accomplish anything for Medgar like this.'"

The day after Medgar's assassination, Charles Evers took over the state leadership of the NAACP. In 1969 he was elected mayor of Fayette, becoming the first black mayor of a biracial town in Mississippi.

The events of the summer of 1963 had served to "dramatize the Negro plight" more vividly, perhaps, than either King or any of his detractors might have expected. What emerged was a tragic picture of the South, sickened by centuries of racial hatred. Surely it could not go on. The death-throes of that order, however violent and frightening, began to seem inevitable: "the American Negro..." King wrote, "has been swept in by what the Germans call *Zeitgeist,* and with his black brothers of Africa and his brown and yellow brothers of Asia, South America, and the Caribbean, he is moving with a sense of cosmic urgency toward the promised land of racial justice." Blacks had now faced the worst (or so it seemed) that their oppressors had to offer, and withal had managed to make gains both moral and material. Whatever the cost, there would be no turning back.

A little light began to shine through. On August 28, 1963 more than a quarter of a million people from all over the nation came to Washington, D.C. to gather in peaceful protest against racial intolerance and poverty. The crowd— white and black, from all classes of society—converged on the city in buses, cars, and on foot, a sea of humanity that swept all the way from the Washington Monument to the uppermost steps of the Lincoln Memorial.

"One cannot help but be impressed," said President Kennedy, "with the deep fervor and the quiet dignity that characterizes the thousands who have gathered in the nation's capital...to demonstrate their faith and confidence in our democratic form of government."

"Faith and confidence" were not always in evidence, however. Several black leaders gave bitter speeches, expressive of the hard road that blacks had travelled, and would still have to travel, in order to obtain their basic human rights. "[Many black] leaders," reported The New York Times, "...spoke in tough, even harsh, language. But paradoxically, it was Dr. King—who had suffered perhaps the most of all— who ignited the crowd with words that might have been written by the sad, brooding man enshrined within."

Ralph Abernathy, a leader of the SCLC, remembers the inspired spontaneity of King's speech: "It is the usual custom of a preacher as he finishes a prepared text to say some other words. Here he establishes eye contact with his audience. On this day, Martin Luther King's speech really began when he left his text. He said, 'I have a dream,' in a

very musical voice, and he lifted his hands in oration. As he lifted his hands, the people lifted theirs, and he went on."

I have a dream..." [A great roar rose up and then gradually dwindled as the crowd listened intently.] "I have a dream that one day on the red hills of Georgia, the sons of former slaves and the sons of former slave owners will be able to sit down together at the table of brotherhood.

I have a dream... [The crowd roared.] ...that one day even the State of Mississippi, a state sweltering with the heat of injustice, sweltering with the heat of oppression, will be transformed into an oasis of freedom and justice.... I have a dream that my four little children will one day live in a nation where they will not be judged by the color of their skin but by the content of their character....

NAACP LEADER MEDGAR EVERS, WHO WAS ASSASSINATED OUTSIDE HIS HOME IN JACKSON, MISSISSIPPI IN JUNE 1963.

As King spoke, the crowd rose to its feet in a thunderous crescendo. Thousands stood on their seats, shouting "Amen!" Finally, his voice booming over the vast emotional uproar, King closed with the words of a Negro spiritual:

"Free at last! Free at last! Thank God almighty I'm free at last!"

Only two weeks after the March on Washington, Alabama Governor George Wallace (whom King called "perhaps the most dangerous racist in America today") closed Birmingham schools to prevent court-ordered integration. Reminiscent of the circus staged in Mississippi a year before, Wallace stationed himself in front of the University of Alabama registrar's office (one arm outstretched in photogenic defiance) to prevent the enrollment of two black women. Robert Kennedy had instructed his liaison in Alabama to treat Wallace "as a joke"—a tactic that seemed appropriate in theory, but which in effect backfired.

Millions of television viewers watched as the ostensibly "amused" justice department official remonstrated with Wallace, or just smirked, while the governor took the opportunity to give a lecture on states' rights. And, of course, the usual cretinous mob had gathered to clap and holler its approval. The two black women stared at the ground in humiliation. They were finally enrolled, but it was a repulsive spectacle all around: a show of irresolution by the United States government that encouraged further insolence from Wallace, and was followed almost immediately by tragedy.

Five days later a black church in Birmingham was bombed and four children killed while attending Sunday school. The outgoing mayor put the blame on Robert Kennedy, for having "forced" integration on an unwilling community: "I hope that every drop of blood that's spilled [Kennedy] tastes in his throat, and I hope he chokes."

For blacks it was an occasion of almost crushing despair. "I can remember thinking," said Dr. King, "that if men were this bestial, was it all worth it? Was there any hope? Was there any way out?"

Nor did such horror deter Bull Connor and his men from lapsing into their old sadism, which, if nothing else, at least gave blacks an even greater moral upper hand. When 3000 black protesters marched to a prayer meeting from the Sixteenth Street Baptist Church, where the bombing had taken place, their path was blocked by a phalanx of policemen led by Connor. King remembered the episode as "one of the most fantastic events of the Birmingham story":

> When [the protesters] refused Connor's bellowed order to turn back, he whirled and shouted to his men to turn on the hoses.... [The protesters], many of them on their knees, stared, unafraid and unmoving, at Connor's men with the hose nozzles in their hands. Then, slowly the Negroes stood up and advanced, and Connor's men fell back as though hypnotized, as the Negroes marched on past to hold their prayer meeting. I saw there, I felt there, for the first time, the pride and the power of nonviolence.

The Civil Rights Act of 1964, proposed by President Kennedy almost 15 months before, was at last signed into law by Lyndon Johnson on July 2. It outlined a three-stage approach to the enforcement of desegregation, relying first on voluntary compliance, then on intervention by state or local authorities, and finally ("when others cannot or will not do the job") federal intervention.

The tone of President Johnson's announcement was that of almost desperate entreaty, reflecting the sense of dread that prevailed after so many tragedies:

> [Americans] believe that all men are entitled to the blessings of liberty—yet millions are being deprived of those blessings, not because of their own failures but because of the color of their skin. The reasons are deeply imbedded in history and tradition and the nature of man. We can understand without rancor or hatred how this all happened. But it cannot continue.... My fellow citizens, we have come now to a time of testing. We must not fail. Let

© Wide World Photos

GANDHIAN PACIFIST
MARTIN LUTHER KING
MEETS MILITANT
BLACK NATIONALIST
MALCOLM X, MARCH
26, 1964. THEY HAD
ONE THING IN COM-
MON—NEITHER
WOULD SURVIVE THE
DECADE.

us close the springs of racial poison. Let us pray for wise and understanding hearts. Let us lay aside irrelevant differences and make our nation whole.

Dr. King planned a massive direct-action campaign to test southern compliance, pointing out that six southern cities—Birmingham, Tuscaloosa, Montgomery, Selma, and Gadsden in Alabama, as well as Albany, Georgia—had indicated that they would flout the law. The week before, riots had broken out in St. Augustine, Florida when a white mob attacked blacks marching in support of the law, which many local businessmen had vowed to disregard. Again, the federal government was called upon to intervene and, finally, the St. Augustine Chamber of Commerce announced its capitulation: "[We will] abide by the law of the land…even

though our group was unanimous in their objections to the public accommodations sections of the bill."

Predictably it was in Alabama, under the stewardship of Governor Wallace, that blacks met with the most resistance. They were not permitted to vote. Blacks would stand in line at polling stations waiting to register, only to be told at the end of the day to "try again tomorrow." Or else their applications would be "lost," or dismissed on some technicality. In Selma, an individual wishing to register needed two voters to "vouch" for him or her. Since no blacks were registered voters, and no white person would vouch for a black person, no blacks were able to vote in Selma.

In March 1965, demonstrators twice tried to march from Selma to Montgomery in support of black voting rights. Both attempts failed. The first time Governor Wallace dispatched state troopers to the Edmund Pettus Bridge at Highway 80, where demonstrators were beaten and teargassed into submission. This coincided with a spree of terrorism in Selma by the Ku Klux Klan, during which scores were injured and two killed, including a white unitarian minister who was dragged out of a black coffeeshop and bludgeoned with a two-by-four. When demonstrators gathered a second time at the bridge, and again were blocked by state troopers, they turned back rather than risk further casualties.

As with Birmingham in 1963, the brutal suppression of protests in Selma provoked a national outcry, as hundreds of supporters came to the city to demand an end to the violence. President Johnson went before Congress to introduce voting-rights legislation. And when civil rights leaders mobilized for a third march, 4000 strong, Johnson was again compelled to send in the national guard (as Governor Wallace had warned that Alabama could not afford the expense of "protecting" the marchers).

On March 26, after a five-day march over the fifty-four-mile (86-km) route from Selma, a triumphant procession arrived at the Alabama Capitol in Montgomery. The tension was palpable: the day before, thousands of visitors had caught taxis, trains, buses, and airplanes to get out of town before nightfall.

PROTESTERS MARCH-ING IN SELMA ON BEHALF OF BLACK VOTING RIGHTS ARE BEATEN BACK BY ALA-BAMA STATE TROOPERS.

At the steps of the Capitol, where columns of state troopers stood guard, Dr. King gave a climactic speech expressing scorn as well as an apparently inexhaustible forbearance:

> Alabama has tried to nurture and defend evil, but the evil is choking to death in the dusty roads and streets of this state.... Our aim must never be to defeat or humiliate the white man, but to win his friendship and understanding. We must come to see that the end we seek is a society at peace with itself, a society that can live with its conscience.

Archive Photos

Though Governor Wallace had been seen parting the blinds of his window during the rally, he did not come down to receive the demonstrators' petition. Instead their delegation was met by his secretary, who told them that the Capitol was closed for the day.

Four and a half months later, at any rate, the Voting Rights Act of 1965 was law.

Many blacks wanted no part of the white man's "friendship and understanding," nor even of his "society." They wanted their own society, complete with independent government, law, economy, and culture. Moreover, they thought that King's philosophy of passive resistance was

contemptible, and that King himself—whom such blacks referred to as "De Lawd" and "Booker T. King"—was an Uncle Tom.

For King's part, one of his most urgent themes concerned the growing influence of a "force [in the black community]…of bitterness and hatred [that] comes perilously close to advocating violence." He warned that "[the white establishment's] continued arrogant ladling out of pieces of the rights of citizenship has begun to generate a fury in the Negro….Few white people, even today, will face the clear fact that the very future and destiny of this country are tied up in what answer will be given to the Negro. And that answer must be given soon."

But many blacks had already run out of patience, giving rise to a number of militant black nationalist groups, the most prominent of which was the Black Muslim movement. Elijah Poole, a Georgia-born ex-factory worker, founded Muslimism in 1931, and by the Sixties he commanded absolute obedience from thousands of followers as The Honorable Elijah Muhammad, Messenger of Allah. Black Muslims took an oath to abstain from smoking, drinking, gambling, dancing, cursing, and consorting with white people (particularly of the opposite sex), whom they called "devils." They envisioned an imminent Armageddon in which the white devils would be made to suffer for their oppression of blacks, and in this regard liked to recite a Muslim poem: "One drop [i.e. of African blood] will make you black, and will also in days to come save your soul."

In the early Sixties Elijah Muhammad's most charismatic disciple was the former Malcolm Little, who had discarded his "slave name" to become, as a Muslim, "Malik Shabazz," known publicly as "Malcolm X" (X meaning identity unknown). While still in his teens, Malcolm X had been a bootlegger, pimp, and drug-dealer in Harlem, until he was caught and sent to prison at age 21, where he first heard the teachings of Elijah Muhammad.

> I am a good example of why Islam is spread-ing across the land. I was nothing but another convict, a semi-illiterate criminal….[Elijah

Muhammad's] teachings brought me from behind prison walls and placed me on the podiums of some of the leading colleges and universities in the country. I often think... that in 1946, I was sentenced to eight to ten years in Cambridge, Massachusetts...and the next time I went back to Cambridge was in March 1961, as a guest speaker at the Harvard Law School Forum.

Malcolm X, while at the height of his power in the Black Muslim movement, was unyielding in his condemnation of the "white devils." His own light skin, he often pointed out, was the result of his grandmother having been raped by a white man. "I hate every drop of white blood in me," he said. As an advocate of black separatism, he claimed to prefer "the candor of the southern segregationist to the hypocrisy of the northern integregationist....A devil is a devil whether he wears a bedsheet or a Brooks Brother suit." According to Malcolm X, all of western civilization had been tainted by a "history-whitening process": Christ, he declared, had in fact been a black man; Beethoven, Haydn, and Columbus were examples of other pseudo-whites. White people falsified such details, he claimed, because they could not bear the fact that the African race was fundamentally superior. But the white man's comeuppance was nigh: "The world since Adam has been white and corrupt. The world of tomorrow will be black—and righteous."

Practically speaking, Black Muslims proposed two basic alternatives to an integrated America: either a mass exodus of blacks from "this house of bondage" back to Africa, or else the separation of the United States into two distinct nations, white and black. Furthermore, Muslims felt that it was morally incumbent on white people to help fund the transition: "Since we have given over 300 years of our slave labor to the white man's America," said Malcolm X, "...it's only right that white America should give us everything we need in finance and materials for the next 25 years, until our own nation is able to stand on its feet."

By 1963 the Black Muslims had become divided over the question of political activism, and consequently Malcolm X left the movement to form his own Organization for Afro-American Unity. "The Muslims generally existed outside the civil rights struggle," says writer Larry Neal, then a follower of Malcolm X. "They did not support any political movements outside of their structure. Malcolm, on the other hand, often addressed himself to the struggles of civil rights workers, particularly the so-called militant wing of the movement.... He wanted the nation of Islam to become more involved in the political struggle as activists, and not just as enlightened commentators on the sidelines." There was one thing that the Black Muslims would never tolerate—apostasy—and certainly not that of one so famous as Malcolm X.

On February 21, 1965, Malcolm X was assassinated during a rally at the Audubon Ballroom in Harlem. Standing before a crowd of 400, he had just given the Muslim greeting, *"As-salaam 'alaykum,"* when a disturbance broke out. "Peace, be cool, brother—" were his last words; he was then hit by a barrage of gunfire that knocked him backwards off his feet. As many as three assassins were involved, all black men, one of whom was shot in the leg outside the ballroom and beaten by the crowd.

Malcolm had accepted his doom. Only a few days before, he told a reporter, "I live like a man who's already dead....No one can get out [of the Black Muslims] without trouble, and this thing with me will be resolved by death and violence." Toward the end, he'd sent a postcard to his biographer, Alex Haley, in which he hinted that "coexistence between the races" just might be possible after all.

"It burst like a Mexican piñata stuffed full of statistics about economics, racism, and frustration," wrote Stanley Crouch of the Watts riots in the summer of 1965.

> [The riots] had...to do with younger blacks who were exchanging the southern patience and idealism of Martin Luther King for the braggadocio of Malcolm X, made attractive by the Muslims' self-reliance program. It also said something about the concepts of manhood...that dominated much more

HARLEM'S AUDUBON BALLROOM ON FEBRUARY 21, 1965, SHORTLY AFTER THE ASSASSINATION OF MALCOLM X.

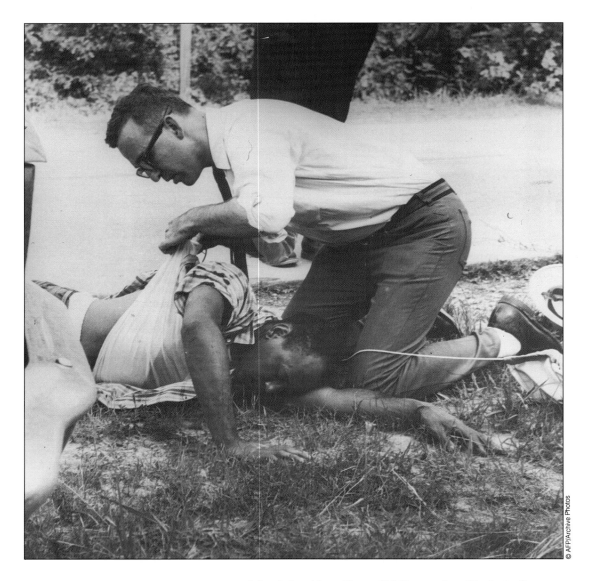

© AFP/Archive Photos

often throughout the rest of the decade: "Burn, baby, burn!" That pretty much said it all—as the Sixties shuddered to a close, many radicals felt that the only solution was to "burn the mother down" and start over.

Though one could hardly have predicted the outcome in terms of sheer atavistic violence, there was a certain inevitability about Watts. Living conditions were, of course, appalling (thanks in part to "Los Angeles' very nearly worthless poverty program," as Crouch, who worked for the program, described it), as was the case with so many black urban areas across the country; further, the mounting rage of black people everywhere was especially intense in Watts, whose residents were regularly brutalized by the Los Angeles police force—the "thin blue line" known even then for its policy of shooting or clubbing first and asking questions later.

The riots might have been started any number of ways, and the deciding factor on August 11 may just as well have been the heat. The story goes, in any case, that a crowd had gathered to watch the arrest of a black man, and the police, in a remarkably ill-advised attempt to frighten them off, singled out a black woman and began to abuse her physically. Things snapped in an instant: the policemen were overwhelmed, run off, and within minutes the scene had erupted, with stones, bricks, and tire irons flying through the air amid a racket of shattering glass. Buildings were set on fire. Store owners fled, and an orgy of joyous looting ensued: "brother assisted brother" in hauling off huge pieces of furniture and appliances; mothers and their children staggered under heavy loads of stolen clothing and other goods; winos reached for Chivas Regal and Johnny Walker Black, tossing the cheap stuff into the flames. When some twenty police cars rolled back into the area in a massive show of force, a blizzard of bricks and bottles pelted them into almost immediate retreat. And for the next day or so, rioters had the place pretty much to themselves.

"It was a bloody carnival," Crouch remembers, "a great celebration. Warring street gangs that had been shooting each other for the past two years were drunk in the park,

television time than did the real suffering of civil rights workers....*Men* did not allow their women to be beaten, hosed, cattle-prodded or blown up in Sunday school. Nonviolence, both as tactic and philosophy, was outvoted.

The conflagration in Watts, a black slum district of Los Angeles, began with the routine arrest of a single man, and ended, three days later, with thirty-five dead, 4000 arrested, and $40 million worth of property damage. Also, a new slogan was coined in Watts, one that would be appropriated by young revolutionaries both black and white, and heard laughing at overturned cars, stoning or stabbing random whites who mistakenly drove through the area, jubilantly shouting how 'all the brothers are together.' There was even hopeful talk about the riot spreading throughout the state, perhaps turning into a full-blown revolution."

On August 14 the National Guard moved in. Watts was cordoned off to a curious public, many of whom stood by and listened to distant screaming and the crackle of gunfire. By the time the revolt had been crushed, the area lay in smoldering ruins. The romantic concept of a black revolution, however, lingered.

Nonviolent activism was practically obsolete by the summer of 1966. On June 7, James Meredith was wounded by a sniper near Hernando, Mississippi as he and a handful of friends conducted a voter-registration march. The next day, some twenty protesters resumed the march from Hernando, and what had begun as a maverick gesture by Meredith ("I was never part of the civil rights movement") was soon transformed into a massive "March Against Fear." Three weeks and 200 miles (320 km) later, a parade of more than 15,000 protesters led by King and other black leaders streamed into Jackson, Mississippi. The march had turned into a mammoth media event, one of the most successful crusades yet—and pretty much the last hurrah of non-violent activism.

Leaders such as Stokely Carmichael of the Student Nonviolent Coordinating Committee (SNCC) and Floyd McKissick of the Congress for Racial Equality (CORE) had agreed to participate in the "March Against Fear" out of deference to King, and hence on his terms. After that, however, they were through with passive resistance. The Meredith shooting had been the last straw. That summer, in Lowndes County, Alabama, Carmichael and John Hulett created the Black Panther party, the stated goal of which was armed insurgency against the white establishment. Their motto was "Black Power."

The concept really blossomed in Oakland, California, where the Black Student Union of Merritt College organized its own Black Panther party in October 1966. Bobby Seale was chairman, Huey Newton the "minister of defense." Newton, who by his own confession was "a meticulous student of every legal aspect of the right of citizens to arm themselves," saw the Black Panthers as "an armed association for community protection against the police." Party members, armed to the teeth, would follow squad cars around black neighborhoods to make sure "the pigs" (their own coinage, soon to become the standard epithet) did not harass black people.

Eldridge Cleaver came to San Francisco in February 1967 to help organize a memorial rally on the anniversary of Malcolm X's assassination. Concerned about security—the Black Muslims had a vendetta against all followers of Malcolm X—Cleaver was directed to Bobby Seale, the man who was "organizing some brothers around guns." Cleaver described his meeting with the Panthers as "literally love at first sight":

"They were in uniforms and brought guns. Black pants, black leather jackets, black berets, powder-blue shirts, black shiny shoes and pretty guns—shotguns, carbines, pistols in holsters…. They were organized and armed, and it made sense…. Huey and Bobby had listened to Malcolm when he called for armed defense teams throughout the United States to deal with those who brutalized the black community."

Cleaver had recently spent nine years in prison, where he wrote an angry testament of black life in America, Soul On Ice. Since then, he'd been writing for the ultra-radical Ramparts magazine. Thus, as an established militant spokesman for blacks, Cleaver was named the Black Panthers' "minister of information," a propagandist role in which, for a while, he proved highly effective.

With Cleaver's shaping of their image, the Panthers became the last word in radicalism. The party had branches in all major cities. The Panther battle-cry, "Right on!" (meaning anything from "Yes, I agree" to "Fire when ready"), was adopted by all kinds of rowdies, black and white. The Panther salute, a raised fist, became the universal symbol of resistance—even more so after two American athletes at

RIGHT: STOKELY CARMICHAEL REPUDIATED NONVIOLENT ACTIVISM IN 1966, COFOUNDING THE FIRST BLACK PANTHER PARTY IN LOWNDES COUNTY, ALABAMA.

OPPOSITE PAGE: A BERKELEY DEMONSTRATOR PUTS UP NO RESISTANCE AS SHE IS DRAGGED AWAY BY POLICE—OBVIOUSLY AN IMAGE FROM THE EARLY DAYS OF THE MOVEMENT.

the 1968 Olympics thrust their fists in the air during the national anthem (a show of "black power" that cost them their medals). Huey Newton became a national folk hero when, in 1968, he was arrested after a shoot-out with the police and thrown in jail. Rallies to "Free Huey" were held all over the country. A poster of Newton, armed with spear and carbine, a scowl of pure menace on his face, was *de rigueur* in the apartments of hard-core radicals everywhere. Bobby Seale liked to call Newton "the baddest nigger ever."

The Black Panthers peaked as a movement toward the close of the decade, then declined just as rapidly. The problem was one of attrition: by the early Seventies dozens of Panthers had been shot dead by the police, and hundreds of their leaders were either in jail or under indictment.

In 1968, while the paramilitary posturing of the Black Panthers kept the nation enthralled, Martin Luther King went on with his work in spite of diminished popular support, low funds, and the constant harassment of the United States government.

"[Nineteen sixty-eight] was a time of increasing desperation for him," recalls Andrew Young, then an adviser to King in the SCLC. "Not only weren't we getting any aid from the federal government, but we had legions of FBI agents tracking us down…trying to disrupt the work we were doing—work which I thought was the only thing that was giving America a fighting chance to survive."

On April 4, 1968, King was in Memphis to lead a rally in support of striking sanitation workers. That evening he stood on his balcony at the Lorraine Motel chatting with friends, asking them to sing a favorite song, "Take My Hand, Precious Lord," at the rally that night. Just then, at 6:01 p.m., he was hit and killed instantly by a slug fired from a flophouse across the street.

Attorney General Ramsey Clark announced within hours of the shooting that a bundle of incriminating evidence had been dropped at the scene, that the culprit would soon be caught, and that the evidence indicated the work of a single, crazed assassin. President Johnson went on television to address the nation, asking "every citizen to reject the blind violence that has struck Dr. King, who lived by nonviolence."

But racial riots had already engulfed more than one hundred American cities. Stokely Carmichael, once a devoted follower of King, was arrested at the head of a mob in Washington, D.C., looting and throwing firebombs. Eldridge Cleaver, who referred to King as a "stumbling block [to the] revolution," was wounded by police two days after the assassination in a gun battle that left Panther Bobby Hutton dead at age 17.

Dr. King had said: "I must face the fact…that America today is an extremely sick nation, and that something could well happen to me at any time. I feel, though, that my cause is so right, so moral, that if I should lose my life, in some way it would aid the cause."

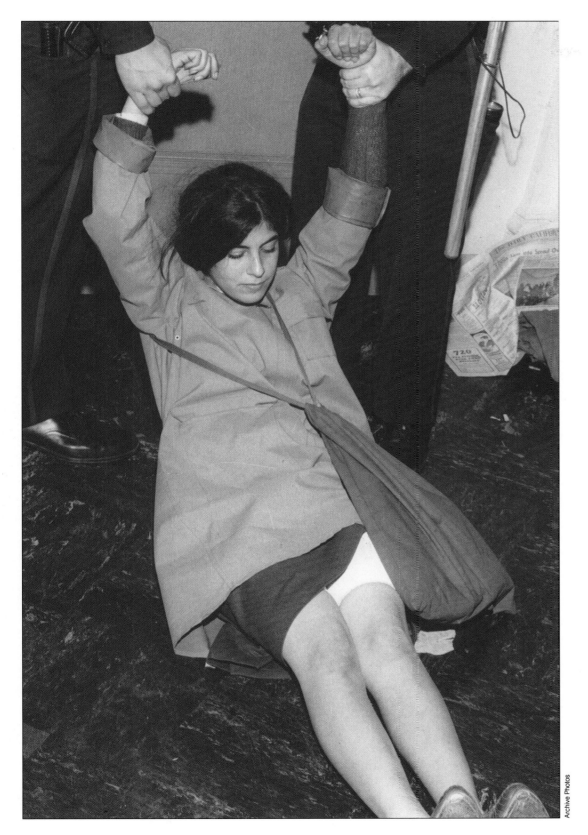

Backround photo: © Wide World Photos; Inset photo: © Peter Gould/FPG International

Archive Photos

Revolt on Campus

The student activism of the Sixties was constructive enough at first. Vietnam had yet to become a large issue, while those of racism, the cold war, and poverty—both at home and in the Third World—provoked a sense of altruism in many young people, who felt themselves more capable than ever of changing the world for the better. In the United States, Kennedy's programs to expand welfare and civil rights, however tentative in practice (and thwarted by Congress), were at least reformist in purpose; and the president's inaugural address ("ask what you can do for your country") served to get the decade off to a properly idealistic start.

The world's ills seemed (to some) so appealingly free of moral ambiguity: surely, racial inequality was wrong; it was good, mutually so, for have-nots to be assisted in some way by those who have; and nuclear annihilation was, after all, to be avoided. And yet, well, there we were, racially and economically polarized, and occasionally on the brink of nuclear war. What were we thinking? Something had to be done, all right. But one was not yet so shrill about things.

Various radical, activist groups that formed during the Sixties came to be known collectively as the "New Left," which encompassed everything from the Black Panthers to the Weathermen to any number of ad hoc "movements" and student revolts that, by the late Sixties, were causing chaos at campuses all over the world.

One of the earliest and most influential of these was Students for a Democratic Society (SDS), organized in 1961 by Tom Hayden, Al Haber, and some of their classmates at the University of Michigan. SDS was formed as a student support network for civil rights workers, though from the start its members wanted to broaden the agenda.

"We believed students could be the catalysts for change in the world," said Hayden. "They were volunteering for the Peace Corps, they were the moving force in the civil rights movement, they were shaking up governments around the world."

THE FREE SPEECH
MOVEMENT OF 1964
AT THE UNIVERSITY
OF CALIFORNIA AT
BERKELEY WAS THE
FIRST GREAT STUDENT
REVOLT OF THE SIXTIES.
HERE, A BERKELEY
STUDENT EXERCISES
HIS FREE SPEECH
"RIGHT" TO USE A
FOUR-LETTER WORD.

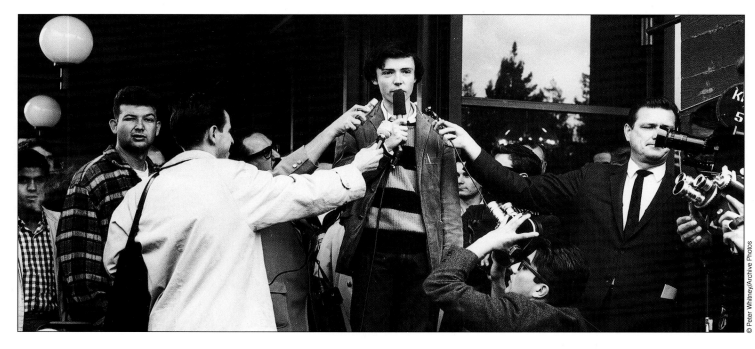

By 1962 there were SDS chapters all over the United States, and a meeting of the newly formed National Executive Committee was planned for June of that year at an AFL-CIO camp in Port Huron, Michigan—a location chosen not for its romantic associations with the old leftist labor movement, but rather due to the fact that SDS received most of its funding from the League of Industrial Democracy and other labor groups. The purpose of the Port Huron convention was to debate the goals of SDS, as well as those of the entire "student movement" (as it was already being called), in order that a coherent manifesto could be drawn up and distributed to whomever in the Establishment would read it. This became "The Port Huron Statement."

Hayden, who wrote the first draft, remembers: "The Port Huron Statement might not seem so radical today, but for 1962 it was a pretty advanced document....We had a concept—'participatory democracy'—that enabled us to begin with immediate grievances and yet aim for more far-reaching changes, thus allowing us to be both reformist and revolutionary. It was a call to action when students wanted to take action."

SDS angered its labor sponsors by, among other things, blaming the United States along with the Soviet Union for starting the arms race—and by just being too radical, period. Funds were summarily cut off and SDS staff-members locked out of their offices. Far from being discouraged, though, SDS members enjoyed their independence from the "old" left-wing and the exhilarating sense of being a new, maverick influence on the national scene. As for the (somewhat tautological) concept of "participatory democracy," it would do as a nominal ideological base, though in effect it amounted to little more than everyone trying to speak at once.

Due in part, perhaps, to the lingering spirit of ultra-Bohemian North Beach (mecca for moody beatniks throughout the Fifties), much of the countercultural turbulence of the Sixties seemed to gravitate toward the San Francisco Bay Area. Thus, during the first half of the decade, before the "left" was aggrandized into the upper-case New Left, the University of California at Berkeley served as, so to speak, the capital of the student movement. Dope-smoking future hippies, guitar-toting folk singers, and budding young revolutionaries with Che Guevaran facial hair became an ever greater presence on campus.

"Even at the beginning of the Sixties there were strange rumblings all around Berkeley," recalls eminent provocateur Abbie Hoffman. "In the fall of 1959, Nikita Khruschev got a rousing reception from thousands as he arrived at his hotel in San Francisco. A United States Air Force colonel's son went on a hunger strike protesting compulsory ROTC. His Pentagon papa showed up to talk him out of it….The House Un-American Activities opened hearings [in May 1960] into alleged subversive activity in the Bay Area."

The proliferation of pamphlet-pushers around Berkeley led to the first great student "revolt" of the Sixties, the Free Speech Movement of 1964. Annoyed by all the pesky radicals at the corner of Bancroft and Telegraph, a spot in front of campus where student politicos typically congregated (with the blessing of the Berkeley police), the administration "discovered" that the property was under university, not city, jurisdiction, and resolved to clear the area. It was rumored that the Berkeley Board of Regents, fairly packed with industrialists and other sinister Establishment types, was at the bottom of this.

Writer/activist Barbara Garson (author of the play *MacBird!*, an LBJ-blasting satire of the Sixties), was herself a fixture at Bancroft and Telegraph:

"But when we returned from our summer vacation in 1964," she remembers, "we were told that we could no longer use the area…Then, very stupidly, [the Berkeley administration] said we could use the space, but we couldn't advocate direct action of any kind. In other words you couldn't say 'Let's go down to the Oakland Tribune and picket.'"

Many students decided simply to ignore the new ruling, and went on setting up tables and handing out leaflets. For a while it seemed as if nothing further would come of it. Occasionally Berkeley officials went to the trouble of collecting students' names, but there was nothing especially threatening about it. Nobody as yet had been forced to vacate the corner. Many students, however, refused to give out their names, often taunting officials either to have them arrested or to lay off entirely, and such little acts of defiance accumulated until finally matters came to a head.

"Jack Weinberg was at the CORE table," Garson says, "when a dean asked his name, which he refused to give. The Berkeley police drove on the campus and put him into a car, and then—hundreds of people claim to have started it—someone sat down in front of the police car so that it couldn't move. Before long, people were all around and over it. Soon Sproul Plaza was covered with thousands of people."

Ordered to disperse, the crowd grew larger. The bemused Weinberg sat in the squad car, which bobbed and creaked as the mob swarmed over it, occasionally ducking to pee into a

A PEACE SYMBOL AND
SMILEY FACE: TWO
PERVASIVE EMBLEMS
OF THE SIXTIES WHOSE
MEANINGS BECAME
MORE IRONIC AS THE
DECADE WORE ON.

bottle someone had given him. The media arrived and the crowd became even more rowdy, realizing they were part of something big. That night, a student named Mario Savio emerged as the leader of what was about to become the Free Speech Movement (FSM). Savio, who had spent the previous summer in the South working for the Student Nonviolent Coordinating Committee, had become all too familiar with petty harassment from the white southern establishment; to return to supposedly enlightened Berkeley and find similar tactics infuriated him.

"It was the classic miracle," Garson recalls, "the boy who stuttered [Savio] stood up on the police car and fluently expressed our deepest sentiments: that our protest was not only for CORE and SNCC but for us students as well.…The university had an entire institute to serve the state's agri-business—and here we were, forbidden to raise nickels and dimes at the campus gates for striking farm workers."

All the following day and night Sproul Plaza was deadlocked, packed with students, while at the center of everything the hapless Weinberg remained in the police car with his bottle. Finally, Berkeley president Clark Kerr—fearing disruption of Family Day, scheduled to begin in the morning—told student delegates that he'd be happy to negotiate with them if they dispersed peaceably. "I argued against dispersal," says Garson, "knowing how much Kerr wanted to avoid an incident, but the crowd acquiesced. Did I think that was a sell-out!"

A sell-out as well as a tactical blunder, it turned out, as Kerr (under the lash of the iniquitous Board of Regents) "constantly betrayed" the students after seeming to make concessions, and finally refused to negotiate at all.

Three months after the Weinberg incident, a massive sit-in took place in Sproul Hall. Savio led the occupation, giving beforehand one of the few memorable speeches of the student movement:

"There's a time when the operation of the machine becomes so odious, makes you so sick at heart, that you can't take part…and you've got to put your bodies upon the gears and upon the wheels and…make it stop."

And with that, some 1,000 students marched into Sproul Hall and sat on the gears. The mood was merry: Christmas carols were sung while folk-fixture Joan Baez strummed her guitar. Eventually the Oakland and Berkeley police came and, rather amiably, arrested some 800 students.

Three days later, with a student strike in effect, President Kerr called an assembly and addressed the students. "We must decide to move ahead or to continue anarchy," he told them. No one had been invited to speak on behalf of the Free Speech Movement, though Kerr had stressed the "togetherness" of the meeting. When Mario Savio attempted to approach the podium, a policeman collared him from behind and dragged him offstage amid roars of protest from the crowd. This public display of brutality appalled both students and faculty alike, the latter of whom had bailed out the sit-in protesters at great cost, and the next day the university senate voted overwhelmingly to accede to FSM demands.

In the end, many students were left feeling more deflated than triumphant, all too aware of the ironic contrast between the principles of their movement and the rather homely reality of what they had won: a few tables on the corner of Bancroft and Telegraph. But at least the Free Speech Movement achieved some kind of tangible victory, which is more than can be said for many of the protests to follow.

Students who became radicalized in the early Sixties through their support of the civil rights movement and other "leftist" causes were ignited into mass revolt by the growing catastrophe of the Vietnam War. As the war's dismal progress was reported nightly on television, modern mass communication making more vivid than ever the human aspect of an otherwise remote conflict, the United States seemed more and more disgraceful for its policy of bloody "imperialist" intervention in a smaller country's struggle for self-determination. "Hey! Hey! LBJ!/How many kids didja kill today?" was the common rallying-cry for young people across the country, who were burning their draft cards and becoming openly and often violently defiant toward authority. Black civil rights leaders, venerated by white student radicals, were emphatic in their denunciation of Vietnam as (in the words of Stokely Carmichael) "a racist colonial war." Even Martin Luther King condemned "the greatest purveyor of violence in the world today—my own country."

As writer Annie Gottlieb put it: "[The] image of the Vietnam War the black movement taught its white apprentices was that of a big armed white country beating up poor Asians, who were heroically resisting."

What amounted to a worldwide "student revolution" broke out in 1968, a year in which campuses throughout the United States, Germany, France, Italy, Britain, and Japan were paralyzed by protest. The "Tet Offensive" in January had suggested that, contrary to optimistic Pentagon reports, the Vietcong were as resilient as ever and that the loss of life on both sides was futile, senseless. But the war went on, escalated; to much of the world, especially the young, the United States became anathema—emblematic not only of its own corruption, but that of all authority, whether it be in government or in the university, on any scale, everywhere.

To protest United States military bases in Japan, thousands of helmeted, club-wielding students poured through the streets of Tokyo, resulting in high-casualty riots with police and pedestrians. The shooting of a student leader in Germany threw the country into an uproar, sparking a series of protest marches in which students waved posters of such New Left heros as Che Guevara, Ho Chi Minh, Lenin, and Rosa Luxembourg. Much of Paris became a militarized zone in May, following the brutal suppression of a demonstration at the Sorbonne (the University of Paris). With broad support from the Parisian citizenry, students and laborers combined forces to take over the university, as well as several factories and most of the Latin Quarter, putting up barricades in defiance of the police. Amid talk of revolution, epic battles were fought through May and June. Then, abruptly, the insurrection collapsed; but the people's faith in De Gaulle's government had been irreparably shaken.

Defeated in a referendum vote, De Gaulle resigned the following year.

In the United States, 1968 was pretty much the nadir of a decade gone very sour. Lyndon Johnson was on his way to becoming perhaps the most reviled president in history; after nearly losing the New Hampshire primary to the obscure Eugene McCarthy, he announced his withdrawal from the race on March 31. A few days later Dr. King was assassinated—news to which Chicago Mayor Richard Daley reacted by ordering his police to "shoot to kill all arsonists." Throughout, the campus served as an apt microcosm for the disintegration of American society.

UBIQUITOUS PEACENIK JOAN BAEZ POPS UP IN GERMANY FOR A BAN THE BOMB RALLY, APRIL 1966.

© Wide World Photos

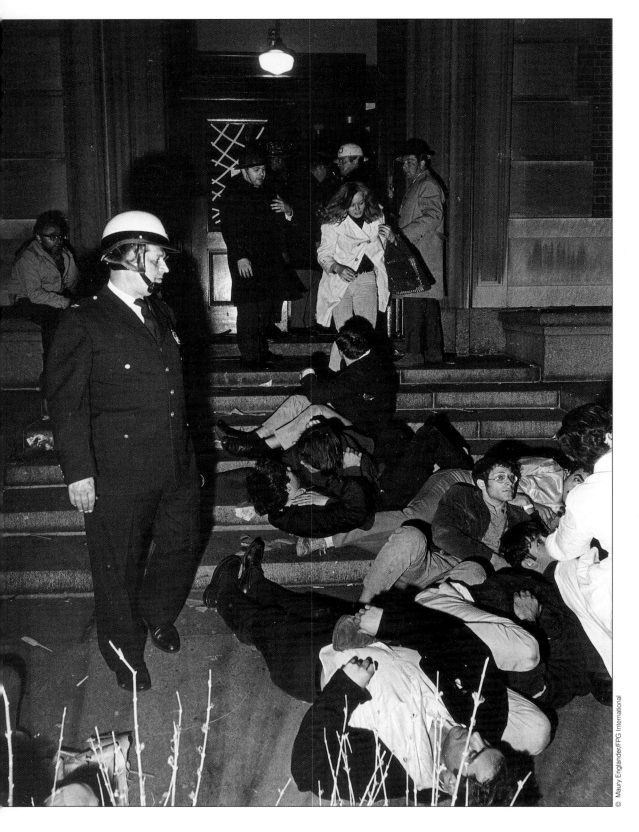

At Columbia University things had been heating up for some time. Its very location, a squalid urban area with Harlem forming its border, was cause enough for tension, which Columbia exacerbated by expanding into black neighborhoods and forcing out residents. Most damning of all was the university's ongoing affiliation with the Institute for Defense Analyses, an organization that conducted military research for the United States government.

As with other major campus revolts, Columbia's began with what seemed a minor incident: on April 22, SDS chairman Mark Rudd and five other students were placed on disciplinary probation for demonstrating inside a university building against regulations. Although the sentence of "disciplinary probation" hardly amounted to Draconian oppression, it was, given the time and place, enough.

Writer James S. Kunen, then a sophomore at Columbia, remembers the strike that ensued:

> Rudd was never particularly revered on campus. He didn't have much charisma, to put it mildly. . . . Nevertheless, the action against him provoked another demonstration, at the Sundial. A rally at the Sundial was quite theatrical, a central event on campus. . . . After a few false starts, the rally moved en masse to Hamilton Hall in order to show solidarity with Rudd and the others by demonstrating inside a building, and then the crowd simply stayed there. We were still there the next morning when The New York Times came out—and we were on the front page. It was a shock—society was paying attention to us! The strike was on its way.

As was the case at Berkeley and elsewhere, student demonstrators were galvanized by publicity, which helped to assure them that they were somehow making a difference—and, of course, they enjoyed the celebrity, the glamor of being perceived as "revolutionaries."

Thus validated by The New York Times, strikers gleefully stayed put in Hamilton Hall, making speeches and gaining in righteous fervor. When they did leave, it was neither the university nor the police who managed to evict them, but rather black students who wanted Hamilton for themselves, and had no patience for white "revolutionary" posturing—a mood that reflected the separatism of the black movement at that time, especially in the wake of King's assassination.

"We had our full share of white guilt," says Kunen, "so we left [Hamilton]—and headed for Low Library, the university administration building. Someone…smashed the glass in the door, opened it, and we ran straight for President Grayson Kirk's office.

"I was excited and nervous. The classroom building, Hamilton, was ours in a way, but the president's office was the inner sanctum—beautiful carpets…a $450,000 Rembrandt on the wall—and Kirk was extremely remote. If you saw him three times in four years it was amazing, and then he was either getting in or out of a limousine."

When the president's office became too crowded, strikers spread out to other buildings, piling furniture against the doors and taunting police and non-striking students outside from open windows. They wore red armbands and waved red flags. Tom Hayden arrived from Newark, where he had been organizing for SDS, and in the spirit of "participatory democracy" formed food, blanket, and press committees and coordinated the nonstop speechifying.

Finally, after a nerve-frazzling—hot, crowded, dull—week of occupation, the police moved in. Kunen recalls:

> Information filtered in via walkie-talkie and runner, descriptions of people being dragged by their hair down stairs, clubbings, blood being spilled…[Ours] was the last building to be emptied. We were prepared to resist. We coated the steps with green liquid soap so the cops would slip….Suddenly I could see five helmets bobbing outside. They were swearing and grunting, working at cutting hoses and ropes around the door, pulling the furniture down piece by piece. I thought when they got me, they'd kill me. People up and down the stairwell were beating a rhythm on overturned wastebaskets….The police grabbed me and broke through our

linked arms. Then, holding on to my feet and arms, they threw me under a tree.…An enormous crowd, densely packed, shouted, 'Strike! Strike! Strike!' with their hands in Vs waving back and forth in the air.

What had begun as a protest over the token punishment of a few SDS members—amplified by hype and mass-hysteria into a protest over any number of muddled "radical" grievances—finally became a protest with a specific, visceral basis: police brutality. This amounts to a virtual paradigm for most, if not all, campus protests of the Sixties. At Columbia, anyway, three more demonstrations were held in reaction to the first police-bust, ending finally in a typical climax of violence followed by mutual puzzlement over the purpose of it all.

"The last [demonstration] was the most violent and terrifying of the three," Kunen concludes, "but like the whole experience, it was unsatisfying—we didn't end the war, and it seemed we succeeded in changing Columbia's policies only in a cosmetic way."

A year after the Columbia riots, black students at Cornell called upon the faculty to institute a Black Studies program, which meant expunging everything that they, the students, perceived as elitist, sexist, and racist about the existing curriculum. The faculty—held literally at gunpoint—agreed to make the changes.

Armed black students, with nearly unanimous support from black faculty members and much of the white student majority, threatened the lives of individual professors as well as those of other black students who refused to take part in demonstrations; hostages were taken, buildings occupied (by then a routine tactic among campus protesters), and the president of the university was physically assaulted.

This time, rather than risk an all-out confrontation—what might have amounted to campus war in the actual sense—student militants were appeased. But it should not have been difficult, at that point, to see where things were heading.

On May 4, 1970 National Guardsmen opened fire on student demonstrators at Kent State University in Ohio,

POLICE EXPEL STUDENTS FROM AN OCCUPIED CAMPUS BUILDING DURING THE COLUMBIA UNIVERSITY STUDENT STRIKE, APRIL 1968.

OHIO NATIONAL
GUARDSMEN MOVE IN
AFTER FIRING ON STU-
DENT DEMONSTRA-
TORS AT KENT STATE.
FOUR STUDENTS DIED
IN THE ATTACK.

hitting 13 people and killing four. The students at Kent State, who had "a distinct reputation for apathy," according to The New York Times, had been demonstrating against the expansion of the war into Cambodia. Two nights before the shooting, the ROTC building had been burned to the ground, and SDS members were threatening to destroy the campus if their demands were not met. The Guard was called in and martial law declared.

The day of the incident, a platoon of armed guards-men fired tear-gas canisters into a crowd of about 1,000 students, who had defied orders to disperse. Chanting "Pigs off campus," several students scooped up the smok-ing canisters and hurled them back, along with stones and chunks of pavement. Guardsmen moved away from the crowd to the top of a hill—turned, formed a line, and fired.

As the Times reported: "Some of the students dived to the ground, crawling on the grass in terror. Others stood shocked or half crouched, apparently believing the troops were firing into the air.…Near the top of the hill…a student crumpled over, spun sideways and fell to the ground, shot in the head.…A young man cradled one of the bleeding forms in his arms.…"

"This should remind us all once again," said Nixon, "that when dissent turns to violence it invites tragedy."

Over a million students on 448 campuses around the country went on strike to protest the Kent State shootings. But protesters seemed to have lost heart, and most of the strikes ended within a few days. Nor were they revived when, less than two weeks later, two black students were killed and twelve wounded at Jackson State in Mississippi.

Guerilla Protest

"A Yippie," said Abbie Hoffman, "is a hippie who's been hit on the head."

In the early days of the Movement, antiwar protesters tried to set a good example, to be the antithesis of the "fascist" Establishment: hence they held sit-ins, sang folk songs, gave interminable speeches, and rarely resisted when the cops came around to drag them away. As for hippies, they may have disavowed the Establishment, but of course they were utterly mellow about it: smoking dope, dropping acid, preaching free love, and pondering Oneness. Meanwhile, the war in Vietnam escalated, demonstrators were brutalized, and the Haight-Ashbury "love generation" imploded with the Summer of Love, itself a sort of ultimate bummer.

Certain factions of the New Left, both on and off campus, were getting mighty tired of the whole pacifist trip—and that included "flower power," "Gandhian" civil disobedience, and all the leftist theorizing. Not only had such methods proved ineffectual as far as ending the war was concerned, they weren't any fun. After all, a mellow lifestyle did not a revolution make, nor did any number of speech-ridden sit-ins. And folk music, with all its morose idealism, was simply dull—*pace* Woody Guthrie, guitars did not really "kill fascists." Fascists had to be confronted, "freaked out." According to Yippie co-founder Jerry Rubin, the new countercultural hero needed to be violent and depraved, a person whose mind had been blown by drugs and rock and roll: "a streetfighting freek [sic], a dropout, who carries a gun at the hip. So ugly that middle-class society is frightened by how he looks. A longhaired, bearded, crazy mother whose life is theater, every moment creating the new society as he destroys the old." Or, if you prefer, a hippie who's been hit on the head.

Rubin, a native of Cincinnati, chucked an abortive career in journalism to join the Berkeley Free Speech Movement in 1964, becoming that most reviled of Establishment foes, the "outside agitator." From the beginning his methods were

extreme: as cochairman of the Vietnam Day Committee in 1965, he led a group of students and dropouts in blocking a train of soldiers en route to the Oakland Army Terminal; he greeted General Maxwell Taylor by building a hedge of barbed wire around the general's limousine. The Establishment was not amused. In 1966 the House UnAmerican Activities Committee (HUAC) decided to crack down on all elements of the antiwar movement, whether passive, violent, or just plain zany.

"HUAC intended to scare everybody to death with… subpoenas," Rubin recalls, "a tactic that worked well against 'communists' in the Fifties. But what passed as a trauma in most places became an honor in Berkeley." Rubin, of course, was among those honored with a subpoena. "The people who got subpoenas were heroes. Those who didn't had 'subpoenas envy.' Everyone wanted one, because they flew us to Washington, put us up in a hotel, and all we had to do was defend our beliefs."

For HUAC the hearings were an unmitigated disaster, the beginning of the end. The various dissident groups in

ABBIE HOFFMAN, YIP-
PIE EXTRAORDINAIRE,
SEPTEMBER 1968.

© Wide World Photos

attendance, from student agitators to Progressive Labor and other leftist groups, gave the committee no respect whatever. Witnesses threatened to vomit on committee members. Unsolicited diatribes on "racist/fascist" America were given. One after another, witnesses were dragged off kicking and screaming. The press, cowed by HUAC throughout the McCarthy era, hence eager to get a bit of their own back, had a field day. For his part, Rubin showed up dressed as a Revolutionary War soldier, complete with blue cutaway coat, knee breeches, and tricorn hat. As it turned out, however, he was unable to testify, as the hearings were cut short after "four foolish days." Rubin says:

> [HUAC] thought they could frighten everyone into submission. But they were dealing with a different situation now. I was from a counterculture. I wasn't trying to keep a job or protect my own economic interest. . . . The hearings were clearly a victory for the antiwar movement. . . . They taught me the power of the media to instantaneously transform public consciousness. And even though I didn't know it at the time, for me it was the start of 'Yippie'—guerilla-theater media politics.

Self-styled "guerillas" came out in force for the "March on the Pentagon" in October 1967, their ranks fortified by a legion of renegade hippies from the Haight, whose peace-and-love wimpiness had been dispelled by the Summer of Love debacle a few months before. Even the supposed moderates were cutting up rough. Dr. Benjamin Spock, the grandfatherly pediatrician, told an angry mob at the Lincoln Memorial that Lyndon Johnson was "the enemy": [He] whom we elected as a peace candidate in 1964, and who betrayed us within three months, who has stubbornly led us deeper and deeper into a bloody quagmire in which uncounted hundreds of thousands of Vietnamese men, women and children have died, and 13,000 young Americans, too." Organizer David Dellinger, a fifty-two-year-old Yale graduate who had been active in the pacifist movement for three decades, declared the rally "a new stage in the American

peace movement in which the cutting edge becomes active resistance."

Whooping youngsters took their cue, running headlong into a cordon of armed soldiers outside the Pentagon, and then, though beaten back by rifle butts and billy clubs, coming back for more! The soldiers hardly knew what to make of it; some of them simply stood there, gaping, as the crowd pelted them with eggs and bottles, howling obscenities. Among the hundreds arrested for disorderly conduct were such unlikely belligerents as the Reverend John Boyles, an Episcopal chaplain at Yale; Mrs. Dagmar Wilson, a founder of the Women's Strike for Peace; and

Archive Photos

(perhaps not so unlikely) Norman Mailer, the novelist, whose account of the march, Armies of the Night, would win the Pulitzer Prize the following year.

But the March on the Pentagon was innovative not so much for its violence as for its weird pageantry, the protesters' sense of theater—that is, their aggressive use of the news media to mock and embarrass the system. Hippies panhandled outside foreign embassies. The National Mobilization Committee to End the War in Vietnam, which organized the event, distributed huge two-sided placards with such pleasantly jingoistic sentiments as BOMB PEKING or one side, and (when the cameras moved in) DOES LBJ SUCK? on the other. Most telling was a climactic demonstration by the Fugs, a provocateur hippie rock group from New York's East Village. Chanting "Out, demons, out," the Fugs attempted to "levitate" the Pentagon and expel its evil spirits; that failing, several protesters broke through lines and urinated on the Pentagon wall.

Thus inspired, the Youth International Party (YIP) was formed two months later, on New Year's Eve 1967, by Abbie Hoffman, Jerry Rubin, and Realist editor Paul Krassner. The "Yippie," Rubin explained, was "the new man born smoking pot while besieging the Pentagon."

The Yippies wasted no time getting noticed. Early the next year at a Democratic fund-raiser at the Hilton Hotel in New York, unwitting party faithfuls were served by a band of Yippie guerillas disguised as waiters. The dinner went pleasantly until the last course—when the waiters emerged stark naked, bearing pigs' heads on platters. While such honored guests as Senators Fulbright and Muskie stared blankly at their desserts (which stared blankly back), Yippies pranced about yelling, "Rome wasn't destroyed in one day!"

Such gross-out tactics appalled not only the Establishment but much of the antiwar movement. Young people who were "Clean for Gene [McCarthy]," a cause for which they had made the ultimate sacrifice—cutting their hair and shaving their beards off, or wearing long dresses instead of minis—felt that Yippies gave all peaceniks a bad name. Many diehard hippies agreed: the Yippies' sordid attacks on

the system gave them bad vibes. "This shocks me and alienates my spiritual sensitivities," said Timothy Leary.

The Yippies couldn't have cared less. They weren't out to win votes, and they certainly weren't about to cut their hair and clean up. They wanted to blow minds, those of "fascists" as well as, if need be, peaceniks—the more the merrier. And before long, other hardcore types wanted to join the fun. YIP being an "international" party, English rebels wanted to know how they might participate. Yippies suggested they dump ten truckloads of cow manure at 10 Downing Street; then, as Prime Minister Harold Wilson came out to inspect, the Anglo-Yips were advised to swallow large hunks of bacon with strings attached, then pull them out of their stomachs while the PM watched. This was given due consideration, but finally abandoned as "impractical."

By the time of the Democratic National Convention in August, the Yippies were pretty much calling the shots among the anti-war faction. A counter-convention had been planned for Lincoln Park called "A Festival of Life," to protest the "Convention of Death" going on at Chicago's International Amphitheater. The hippies of the city's bohemian North Side wanted to organize their convention on the lines of the San Francisco Be-In the year before, with free music, free love and dope, and good vibes galore, but the Yippies changed all that. They argued that such a demonstration was passé, that it might earn them a paragraph in the newspapers but no more. They suggested a new theme for the counter-convention: "Freak out the Democrats while the whole world watches." This meant, or so it was rumored, that Yippies would pollute Chicago's water supply with LSD; that they would disguise themselves as bellboys and molest delegates' wives in their hotel rooms; that they would paint their cars yellow and taxi unsuspecting democrats into remote Illinois farmlands.

None of this came to pass exactly, though plenty else did. On the first day of the convention—which happened to be Lyndon Johnson' sixtieth birthday—the Fugs threw an "anti-birthday party" at the Chicago Coliseum to "freak out the biggest freak of all." This "high-decibel, multi-media

party" reminded reporter J. Anthony Lukas of "another event held long ago in [the Coliseum]: "The 'first ward ball,' sponsored by the unsavory ward leaders, Michael (Hinky Dink) Kenna and John (The Bath) Coughlin, and attended by some of the city's most renowned athletes, gamblers… prostitutes, pickpockets and racketeers." The Fugs described the party as a "tribute to Mr. Johnson's historic career all the way from the first election he stole in Texas to the new anti-personnel weapons his Administration has developed for use in Vietnam and the ghettos." In this spirit, the Holocaust No-Dance Band ripped through such numbers as "Master of Hate" (written in honor of LBJ), while partygoers milled past strobe-lit pictures of slaughtered Vietnamese civilians and refugees fleeing their burning huts.

Meanwhile packs of Yippies roamed the streets of Chicago, looking for opportunities to strike. Despite the vigilance of Mayor Daley's police force, the guerillas managed to spread dog droppings around the lobby of the Hilton, toss stink bombs into the Go Go Lounge at the Palmer House Hotel, and, most triumphantly, overrun the statue of General John Logan in Grant Park and raise the Vietcong flag—a picture that made the front pages of newspapers all over the world.

That night, the "alternate delegation" congregated in Lincoln Park to nominate their own presidential candidate: "Pigasus," a live pig. At 11 P.M., the park closed, and a gathering swarm of policemen ordered the 3,000 protesters to disperse. Amid chants of "Hell no, we won't go," picnic tables were turned over, trash baskets full of paper and wood piled between the upturned legs, and all of it set on fire, forming a flaming barrier between protesters and police. Patrol cars slowly circled the area, their spotlights cutting through the smoke and passing over a jumble of contorted faces and jabbing middle fingers. Protesters clapped, shouted, waved Vietcong flags, and taunted the police. "Why don't you go home to your kids?" one of them shouted. "While you still have them," shouted another.

With that, some 300 policemen snapped down their visors and charged.

ABBIE HOFFMAN AT THE 1968 DEMOCRATIC NATIONAL CONVEN-TION IN CHICAGO.

AT THE DEMOCRATIC CONVENTION YIPPIES TRY TO DRUM UP SUPPORT FOR THEIR CANDIDATE, "PIGASUS," A LIVE HOG. A FEW MONTHS LATER, PIGASUS' "INHOGURATION" TOOK PLACE NEAR PRESIDENT NIXON'S IN WASHINGTON, D.C.

Abe Peck, then editor of The Seed, Chicago's underground newspaper, remembers the confrontation: "The helmeted wave flowed across the park, lofting tear gas and smoke bombs and waving nightsticks over their heads. They had no use for the 'peacecreep dope-smoking faggots,' and they told us so with a scream that said it all. 'Kill! Kill! Kill!' When they were about 25 yards away, most of us took the hint. Some of us didn't take it fast enough. 'Walk! Walk!' said the ever-concerned clergy before they were smashed to the ground. 'Help! Help!' screamed a girl as the police tossed her into the park lagoon….The battling swirled into the streets of Old Town. Passersby were clubbed as they opened the doors to their own homes. Pistols were fired—only into the air, by the grace of God."

As Chicago's Finest flailed away at everything in sight, and cameramen recorded it all for the evening news, a chant welled up out of the chaos: "The whole world is watching! The whole world is watching!"

The Yippies had gotten their wish.

"The Inauguration weekend," wrote Hunter S. Thompson, "was a king-hell bummer in almost every way. The sight of Nixon taking the oath, the doomed and vicious tone of the protest, constant rain, rivers of mud, an army of rich swineherds jamming the hotel bars, old ladies with blue hair clogging the restaurants…a horror-show for sure."

Those of the antiwar movement, with all their frenzied vilification of LBJ, Hubert Humphrey (or "The Hump" as Yippies called him, in a spirit of almost affectionate ridicule), and the Democrats, hadn't known how good they'd had it. Now arch-conservative, arch-repressive Nixon was president. That took the wind out of the New Left and put things in very bleak perspective: while they had bashed away at poor, hobbled LBJ, the Nixon specter had drifted by all but unregarded. And now he was here—he was back.

The counter-inauguration march revealed the shape of things to come for the antiwar movement. Although most protesters marched peacefully enough—even listlessly (their "mood appeared dampened," noted The New York Times, "by the prospect of Mr. Nixon's presiding over the liquidation of the war")—a small hardened core of protesters, a few hundred out of the thousands who participated, went on a spree of random nihilistic violence. They smashed windows at several banks (to get at "capitalist pigs," presumably); they smashed windows at the Smithsonian and the National Geographic Society; they smashed the windows of police and civilian cars alike, sometimes wrenching off the hoods and severing ignition wires; they went after police with clubs and rocks, seriously injuring three and getting beaten senseless themselves; they hauled down and burned American flags; and they fought with other protesters who tried to restrain them.

David Dellinger of the National Mobilization Committee dismissed such people as "crazies," but added: "However, I can understand their anger and frustration."

The march proper was an odd mixture of rage and resignation. Some of the banners read WE MISS BOBBY, referring to Robert F. Kennedy, whose candidacy had ended with his assassination six months before, as well as PEACE NOW and JOIN US. The rest of the banners, however, were comprised of endorsements for the Vietcong and scabrous attacks on the new administration, as in (one of the mildest), NIXON'S THE ONE [the Republican campaign slogan]—THE NUMBER ONE WAR CRIMINAL. The chants were mostly obscene or vicious: "Two, four, six, eight/Organize and smash the state!" and "Ho, Ho, Ho Chi Minh/the N.L.F. is going to win!" The Yippies' "guerilla-theater" tactics were still in evidence, but already the playful "theater" aspect of guerilla protest was on its way out (along with YIP itself): a few wore Nixon masks, pretending to pick their nose throughout the twenty-block distance of the route; and at the end of the march, a counter-inaugural ball was held in a tent near the Tidal Basin, an area so muddy that protesters' shoes were sucked off their feet. It was here that, fittingly enough, the "inhoguration" of Pigasus took place.

The Students for a Democratic Society had come a long way since their quaint Port Huron salad days. By the time of the SDS national convention in June 1969, those of the controlling faction, who called themselves "Wreckers," no

© Wide World Photos

longer thought it possible to work within the system. They regarded the revolution as inevitable, as only a question of when and how. Another faction came to the convention with a position paper titled, "You Don't Need a Weatherman to Know Which Way the Wind Blows," a line taken from one of Bob Dylan's gloomier ballads, "Subterranean Homesick Blues." This faction, like the Wreckers, favored armed insurrection against the state, but they thought the Wreckers themselves were wimps.

In the last, dark days of the Movement, "political correctness" was not a matter of expressing liberal sensitivity through the use and abuse of euphemisms; rather, it was a matter of how committed you were to revolutionary ideals, of the extent to which you were willing to divest yourself of "bourgeois" values, of whether or not you were willing to die, even kill, for the Cause. By such standards, the "Weathermen" faction of the SDS was the most eminently "correct" of all, the *ne plus ultra* of what the antiwar movement had become toward the end of the Sixties.

The motto of the Weathermen (or "Weather Underground," as they came to call themselves, after striking the sexist "men" from their name) was "Bring the war home," which meant armed guerilla strikes against America, in America (which they spelled "Amerika," to suggest Kafkaesque repression). For them, it was far too late for protests, for marches, speeches and sit-ins, and for utopian dreaming about the better world they would someday, somehow make for themselves. All that, they felt, had been wrongheaded from the start: the first priority was to destroy the system, to blow it up, and to kill the pigs (by then, "pigs" meant not only policemen and heads of state, but all those who were deemed bourgeois and "counterrevolutionary"); then, and only then, amid the ashes, did one think about what came next.

After June 1969, the Weather Underground *was* the SDS —they had the membership roster and the bank account in their possession. They had dominated the convention, shouting down all politically incorrect speakers. In a milieu not unlike the Nuremberg rallies of the early Thirties

PROTESTERS WAVE THE
VIETCONG FLAG FROM
ATOP A STATUE OF GEN-
ERAL JOHN LOGAN IN
CHICAGO'S GRANT
PARK.

(different ideology, same ambience), commitment was everything, and theirs was impressive. Weatherpeople literally set out to brainwash themselves through a Maoist process called "criticism/self-criticism," whereby one seeks to purge the mind of all counterrevolutionary notions including any lingering sentimentality about the sanctity of human life. One's own life, after all, was not sacred—it was subordinate to the cause. Having recognized the necessity to kill and be killed, to become a "doomed executioner," in André Malraux's term, one simply made the necessary psychological adjustments.

Weatherpeople planned a bloody "Days of Rage" confrontation for October, on the second anniversary of the slaying of Che Guevara in Bolivia. This apocalyptic event, they decided, would be staged in Chicago where so many of them had become battle-hardened during the 1968 Convention, fighting against Mayor Daley's "stormtroopers." Meanwhile, they set about finding recruits. All college students were out of the question, being inherently bourgeois (Weatherpeople themselves had dropped out), and the working class was too "steeped in racism." That left high school kids, who the Weatherpeople thought were the future "revolutionary class" of America—a great slumbering giant of disaffection, ready to be awakened. Thus the Underground embarked on a series of "jailbreaks" at high schools all over the country, storming into classrooms to announce the liberation of the "prisoners of the Amerikan school system." Teachers who weren't too bewildered to protest were beaten and tied up. Weatherpeople, barking over their shoulders, securing the knots, urged kids to join them outside for a rally, and later in Chicago for the Days of Rage. "Most people thought we were nuts," recalled former Weatherperson Jeff Jones.

On October 8, a grim corps of seventy guerillas marched into Lincoln Park wearing white helmets and jackets with Vietcong flags stitched to the back. There they built a bonfire and awaited the influx of thousands of adolescent freedom-fighters, marching thither from all over the country, the drumbeat of destiny resounding in their downy ears. As it turned out, about 400 people showed up, mostly Weather Underground organizers and a few rowdy youths they'd rounded up from the streets.

Weatherperson Bo Burlingham remembers his arrival at the scene: "As I approached, it dawned on me just how few of us there were. This realization aroused such a tumult in my stomach that I had to force myself to think of other things. I remember what followed as a dream."

A silent, purse-lipped interval of intensive criticism/self-criticism was broken by a ululating whoop, the battle-cry of rebel Algerian women that Weatherpeople had learned from the movie Battle of Algiers. The putsch was on. Two-by-fours aloft, they stampeded out of the park and commenced smashing windows up and down the street, engaging in quixotic battle with lampposts and parked cars along the way, barrelling full-force into the police officers who were sent to try to stop them.

"Suddenly lights flashed and I heard what sounded like a string of firecrackers," Burlingham recalls. "Someone said it was gunfire. A few of us were shot that evening. I remember running, running, running until my sides and throat ached. I wanted to sleep. I felt like vomiting. But I just followed the people in front of me wherever they ran."

After three days of guerilla sorties such as this one, the insurrection was quashed. Scores of Weatherpeople were seriously hurt, as were several police, and one city official was paralyzed from the neck down when he was flattened in the midst of the final engagement in the Loop. Weatherpeople still standing were arrested en masse and thrown in jail, where they waited, for the most part euphorically, until their exasperated parents came to post bond.

A few months later, in February 1970, Weatherpeople Terry Robbins, Diana Oughton, and Ted Gold blew themselves up while trying to make bombs in a Greenwich Village townhouse. As no counterrevolutionaries were harmed in the blast, the only people whom the Underground ever managed to kill in pursuit of the Cause were, in the end, themselves. After that, the Weather Underground went underground for good.

ARTS AND ENTERTAINMENT

Why Art Went Pop

In 1963 New York's Guggenheim Museum held an exhibition of pop art, bringing worldwide attention and a certain degree of legitimacy to a movement that exalted (however ironically) objects such as soup cans and toilets to the realm of high art. Its practitioners took a sort of deadpan pride in their own banality. "A Coke is a Coke," wrote Andy Warhol, whose works include a silkscreen of 112 Coke bottles, "and no amount of money can get you a better Coke than the one the bum on the corner is drinking. All the Cokes are the same and all the Cokes are good. Liz Taylor knows it, the President knows it, the bum knows it, and you know it." If such a pronouncement failed to make one reflect deeply upon an age of rampant consumerism, that was probably okay with Warhol. Blandness was more or less the point.

That pop art is at least somewhat indebted to the work of such abstract expressionists as Willem de Kooning, Robert Motherwell, and Jackson Pollock is perhaps the crowning irony. These painters felt that the creative act involved a struggle to "liberate the subconscious," to depict one's inner

turmoil on canvas. Far from the simplified realism (or "neo-realism," as it were) of pop art, the work of abstract expressionists was free-associative and non-representational. Pollock's method was to dash pell-mell over an unstretched, unprimed canvas, rushing to keep pace with his frantic muse, flinging industrial paint this way and that until everything was just so (though sometimes the odd cigarette butt or nail was necessary for true textural perfection). "I want to express my feelings rather than illustrate them," he said.

By 1965 popster Roy Lichtenstein was mocking the proud spontaneity of Pollock and other so-called "action-painters." His Little Big Painting amounts to a parody of typical abstract-expressionist forms: that is, "impetuous" multicolored slashes are rendered in Lichtenstein's mechanistic, benday-dotted comic-strip style. This may have been the artist's way of saying that all this "liberation-of-the-subconscious" stuff was pretentious hokum. If so, he and other like-minded wags were, in effect, negating the essential *raison d'etre* of twentieth-century art prior to the Sixties.

It may as well be noted that Pollock, at any rate, died in 1956 and so was spared the advent of Lichtenstein and the whole ironical, unexpressive pop movement.

The Guggenheim pop show happened to coincide with the fiftieth anniversary of the 1913 exhibition of modern art at the 69th Regiment Armory in New York City, which had introduced the revolutionary work of Matisse, Kandinsky, Brancusi, Picasso, and Braque to North America. Critics scoffed, but over 250,000 Americans showed up to have a look at the bizarre products of such movements as Cubism, Futurism, Expressionism, and Fauvism, all of which, whatever their theoretical niceties, were bonded by an aversion to realism, favoring instead one's internal conception of a subject. In practice this meant that a man or woman might be depicted with, say, one eye and three noses (Cubism), bald, wavy and howling (Expressionism), elongated and mauve-skinned (Fauvism), or "dynamically" breaking apart (Futurism). An example of the latter was Marcel Duchamp's Nude Descending a Staircase, an experiment in capturing motion on canvas that a skeptical critic re-named Explosion in a Shingle Factory. No matter: the Armory Show firmly established modern art in North America.

World War I convinced modernists that they had been right all along about the equivocal nature of surface reality. Dada, a movement dedicated to the subversion of all traditional values in philosophy and the arts, promoted "automatic" writing and painting, in which logic was suspended and the subconscious allowed (insofar as it was able) to dictate a work of art. In 1920, artists at a Dada exhibition in Cologne, Germany invited viewers to destroy their paintings. This was *l'art pour l'art* at its most pure, in light of which nothing that followed could seem especially farfetched. Enter the "New York School" of abstract expressionists.

"All these years," wrote Tom Wolfe in The Painted Word, "I, like so many others, had stood in front of a thousand, two thousand, God-knows-how-many-thousand Pollocks, de Koonings, Newmans, Nolands, Rothkos, Rauschenbergs, Judds, Johnses…Klines…now squinting, now popping the eye sockets open, now drawing back, now coming closer—waiting, waiting, forever waiting for…IT…for IT to come into focus, namely, the visual reward…."

In theory, abstract artists of the Forties no longer had to be conscious of what they were painting. The subconscious was doing all the work. The painters of the New York School rendered their turmoil either with simplified blocks of color or what appeared to be (to the layman) arbitrary slashes and drips, butts and nails. Some abstract expressionists went to great length to propound a doctrine, or anti-doctrine, behind their visions: "We are reasserting man's natural desire for the exalted," said New York Schooler Barnett Newman, "for our concern with our relationship to the absolute emotions…. We are freeing ourselves of the impediments of memory, association, nostalgia, legend, myth, or what have you, that have been the devices of Western European painting. Instead of making cathedrals out of Christ, man, or 'life,' we are making it out of ourselves, out of our own feelings."

Newman's own sense of the exalted led him to paint huge, solid-colored canvases, with portentous titles like *Day One* (solid red with faint orange trim). To the average viewer such paintings may amount to nothing more than large

JASPER JOHNS, POP ART
ICON OF THE 1960s.

© Archive Photos

blocks of red, blue, or what have you; to the art critic whose business it was to define aesthetic trends, Newman's works were "stark expanses of serene unbroken color…[that] could be read as expressions of infinity and expanse" (so wrote Patterson Sims of the Whitney Museum of Art). One assumes that such pundits cultivated a poker face, but at any rate the source of the later pop artist's irony may now become evident.

Within the New York School there were two loosely definable types: those such as Newman and Mark Rothko who went in for "stark expanses" of color (though Rothko's titles—e.g., Red and Blue over Red; Black, Ochre, Red over Red—were more literal than Newman's), which critic Clement Greenberg called "American-type painting"; and the "Action Painting" of Pollock, de Kooning, and Franz Kline. Kline's best-known work features bold black slashes against a lighter background, creating a sort of calligraphic effect. De Kooning caused a great sensation among his fellow abstractionists by returning, after a fashion, to the human figure as a subject. His Woman series of the early Fifties sought to "explode the female form," proving the aptness of Rothko's claim that, for abstract painters, "a time came when none of us could use the figure without mutilating it." So far as that went, de Kooning succeeded.

The first throbs of what came to be known as Pop Art are found in the work of Robert Rauschenberg and Jasper Johns. Influenced by his versatile predecessor Marcel Duchamp (who went from the "dynamism" of Nude Descending a Staircase to the prophetic Fountain, a proto-pop rendering of a simple urinal), Johns focused in his early work on the American flag, painted in all its literal flagness, un-"exploded" or otherwise mutilated. "The combination of painterly surface richness," explains Patterson Sims, "with the quintessential American icon signalled the transition from Abstract Expressionism to Pop Art."

As a further move back to realism, Rauschenberg began to incorporate such objects as might be found "by tipping over a trashcan" (as Italian pop collector Giuseppe Panza put it), including bottles, stuffed chickens, and bits of old furniture. This was in keeping with what may be considered the definitive aim of pop art—namely, taking commonplace objects out of their usual contexts so that the viewer sees them from a fresh perspective. Still, Rauschenberg continued to emphasize the process of creation over the actual product created, which smacked too much of the old "liberation-of-the-subconscious" manifesto to make him a pop artist proper.

"I was a child of the advertising bombardment," wrote pop pioneer James Rosenquist, who started his career as a sign painter in New York, "and though I hadn't liked the outcome of my [commercial] work…the largeness of it had been a blow to my consciousness. I began to use fragments of realistic images—a huge image of spaghetti, somebody's nose as big as a ski slide with eyes three feet wide."

After fifty years of increasingly whimsical abstractions, many artists who came of age in the Sixties figured there was little else to be done with slashes, drips, and blotches without seeming hopelessly derivative. On the other hand, earlier forms of realism—depending on subtle nuances of light, shade, and color for their effects—had been hashed over for centuries on end and required a great deal of technical skill besides. And subtlety of any sort was apt to be lost on a generation of alienated consumers, their senses pummeled by television and the hubbub of everyday life.

Pop art, then, was the logical (and uniquely American) by-product of such an age: if slashes, drips, and blotches were passé and classical realism not only passé but, for most artists, technically unattainable, and since the twentieth century had made art more a matter of abstruse theory than concrete aesthetic standards, then it was surely valid to paint banal objects of mass-production to parody the banal culture to which such objects belonged. Why not? The idea went no further than the thing itself—*l'objet pour l'objet*.

Yes, a sense of irony was key. As Rosenquist explained it: "[Pop artists] looked for dreams and values that could come from a culture in which everything seemed to be immediately obsolete."

Folk Music

Idealism can be a gloomy business. Say you're a privileged white kid, growing up in the midst of the affluent Sixties, perhaps a student at an expensive private college, not a worry in the world. Do you simply kick back and enjoy the best years of your life? Do you while away the days swooning over the latest throb-and-sob idols on the AM radio, or get smashed with your frat brothers at yet another kegger? When all around you is the sordid evidence of social injustice, hypocrisy, commercialism, and man's inhumanity to man? It don't seem right!

Better by far to declare your solidarity with the "suffering masses," to break free of your bourgeois roots and take to the streets, a guitar slung over your shoulder—a ramblin', rovin' folkie who braves the "cruel winds" in his or her search for a better way. But no amount of slummy Bohemian mortification can ever assuage your middle-class guilt. So you suffer inside, and it shows. If a woman, you emulate folk madonna Joan Baez: you shun makeup, part your hair down the middle and comb it straight—like somber curtains barely drawn—and sing songs about lumpenproletariat lives that end in graves dug "long and narrow"; barefoot, you roam the streets of Greenwich Village in a burlap schmatte, your nose buried in a dog-eared copy of The Bell Jar. If a man, you become a sort of saintly hobo, like "The Freewheelin' Bob Dylan": you drop your g's, wear Iron Boy overalls, a threadbare denim jacket (the better to feel them proverbial cruel winds a-blowin') and a striped engineer's cap—ready, willin' and able to hop a freightcar and yodel your way to that next lonesome town, where a brand new band o' vagabond brothers awaits you.

Such was the mellow, dusky Utopia sought by young, politically correct folksters in the early Sixties, sustained by endless hours of mute commiseration in the coffeehouses of Cambridge, Massachusetts, and Greenwich Village, New York. There they would sit with their java and butts, morose and scrawny (indeed, too sad to eat), attending to some bleakly "relevant" folk anthem—perhaps a splendidly per-

tinent, gloriously uncommercial Gaelic ballad written by, say, famished Irish potato farmers in the seventeenth century.

The folk craze got under way in the late Fifties, as a sort of alternative Bohemianism for those who might otherwise be beatniks, had the latter not been so damn nihilistic, bummed out about the Bomb, and insufferably more-alienated-than-thou. Folkies were depressed, no doubt about it, but the more activist among them were typically young enough to have a few ideals intact. After all, who could listen to Woody Guthrie's "This Land Is Your Land" and not dream of a better tomorrow when people of all classes and races would join hands and march as one toward a glowing, rose-hued horizon?

Saint Woody notwithstanding, the most important watchword among folk enthusiasts was "ethnic": since the heart of folk wisdom had sprung from the suffering masses, and since most of the masses were non WASP (and since

© Lisa Law

BOB DYLAN CROONS ABOUT SOCIAL IN-JUSTICE AT THE LAW CASTLE IN LOS ANGELES, 1965.

WASPs tended to make lame music whether they suffered or not), it was imperative that one seek out the most obscure, authentically ethnic music one could find. This meant haunting the Library of Congress for recordings of Mississippi chain-gang chants; hunkering discreetly at the rear of Pentecostal churches (tape machine rolling) while the Holy Rollers howled; and plumbing the record stacks for ballads of the Lapland seal hunters, for Irish peasant ditties. In short, one dug deep.

The hub of the folk movement was Israel ("Izzy") Young's Folklore Center, opened in 1957 at 110 MacDougal Street in the Village. The Folklore Center carried enough esoterica to fill the heart of even the most hardened purist, though it served as a great deal more than just a music and record store; it organized "hootenannies" (Woody Guthrie's term for a folk music sing-along) and Appalachian-style wingdings servin' cider 'n' cheese refreshments; it distributed Socialist political pamphlets and folk history monographs.

The Center's newsletter was required reading for folkies all over the world. Riddled with typos and smudged by the mimeograph, it was just the sort of honestly amateurish venture that its readers craved. An excerpt from the Autumn 1961 issue:

> Odetta goes to Europe to do TV in Holland, Sweden, France.... Alice Conklin, Theo Bikel's new secretary, was seen at Feenjon's recently, enjoying herself to the guitar work of Steve Knight.... Jack Ballard works full time, seven days a week at the store now. Please do not ask him to sing every time you come into the store.

Other than crucial updates on the whereabouts of Miss Conklin and that gentle admonishment *re* the harried Jack Ballard, there was also in that issue a one-page advertisement announcing "Bob Dylan in his First New York Concert: Saturday, November 4." Bob Dylan (*né* Zimmerman) had arrived in New York earlier that year after his first semester at the University of Minnesota. En route, he'd made a pilgrimage to Woody Guthrie's sickbed at Greystone Park Hospital

in New Jersey, whereupon the torch was passed. Renamed Dylan (after the poet and sainted patron of the White Horse Tavern in Greenwich Village) he set about divorcing himself from the heavy stigma of his white middle-class background, telling Izzy Young in a newsletter interview that he'd spent his childhood as a carnival roustabout, a gypsy, learnin' the blues at the knee of a Chicago street singer.

Dylan became the darling of the folk establishment. The cover of his second album, The Freewheelin' Bob Dylan, secured the image: that of a down-but-not-out, tortured-but-happy ramblin' boy, stragglin' down the snow-muddied, cruelly windy streets of the Village with his girlfriend locked joyously to his arm. One can't help but feel, lookin' at this album cover, that these two youngsters are gonna do okey-dokey, though it's a tough ol' world out dere and one can only hope for the best. "That cover was a symbol of my generation," wrote the wistful Carol Belsky in Bringing It All Back Home. Dylan himself admitted, "The cover is the most important part of the album." The fact that Dylan had a joltingly awful singing voice dint hurt 't'all, no-how: on the contrary, it gave every adenoidal would-be folksinger reason enough to hope that he, too, could become the Voice of a Generation. Besides, it was honest; to sound polished was somehow suspect, decadent, even (the most damning word in the folkie's vocabulary) commercial.

"Sister Mystic and Brother Outlaw," Joan Baez called herself and Dylan during those halcyon Village days in the early Sixties. They all but ruled the place. Baez, especially, had done much to attract earnest college kids during the early days of the boom, espousing a brand of *engagé* folkism so full of morbid urgency that one could hardly fail to be moved by it. She almost never smiled. Her almond eyes seemed forever a-brimmin' with bravely unspent tears. She was clearly very blue about things. How blue was she? At the 1960 Newport Folk Festival, she arrived in a hearse.

In 1961 it seemed like every other Villager under the age of twenty-five had a guitar, banjo, or dulcimer thumping in his or her wake. Every Sunday these kids would swarm around the fountain in Washington Square Park for a massive hootenanny, a squall that upset residents not only because of its noise, but, worse, because of the music's pinko themes—the sort of activity that lured longhaired beatnik pervert-types out of hiding and into the park. The police were called in to put a stop to it. On April 9 (what would go down in folkie history as "Black Sunday"), policemen ordered the singers to desist and disperse. The latter responded with a rousing chorus of "We Shall Not Be Moved." The police, not a folk fan among them, charged—only to be met with fierce resistance in the form of shin-kicking, slapping, and biting, until finally almost every last folkie had to be wrestled into paddy wagons and off to jail ("These cold, cold bars entrappin' me/Yet somewhere, somehow, my heart is free…"), where the hootenanny was punishingly resumed.

The next month, amid rumors that a Right-to-Sing Committee was being formed, Mayor Wagner ordered the folkies back in the park.

That same year Newsweek noted: "Never before have the songs of the shoeless enjoyed so much popularity with the well shod." Heedless of the nice distinction, Newsweek dismissed most folkies as "pure beatniks" (by the Sixties, beatniks had gotten very tiresome), but added approvingly that many connoisseurs were "typically collegiate, devoted to button-down shirts and J. Press suits as well as peace and equality." This, of course, struck an ominous note with folk purists, who prided themselves on being, if not shoeless, very poorly shod (in Fred Braun sandals or Dylanesque engineer's boots). Could it be that their beloved folkiness was being appropriated by popular culture? Commercialism! Irrelevancy! Folkies were adamant: one could not serve two masters, whether they be God and Mammon or, more to the point, Social Justice and J. Press.

But the deluge was on. In 1961, a fateful year, a record 400,000 guitars were sold, falling not only into the righteous hands of true-believin' folkniks but also those of anti-Bohemian Rotarian types, whose idea of a hootenanny was to gather the wife n' kids 'round the Burl Ives Songbook,

a bubblin' pot of fondue at the ready. Such defilers had no time for hobo-types like Dylan, Leadbelly, or the Kweskin Jug Band; they thought it was slummy enough, for goodness' sake, to be strummin' along with the Kingston Trio's harmonized, sterilized version of the old Appalachian ballad, "Tom Dooley." Every Sunday in church throngs of the squeaky-white middle class could look forward to their banjo-totin', g-droppin' minister, leadin' the congregation in a glib rendition of "This Land Is Your Land" (forgetting, for the nonce, Woody Guthrie's commie politics). Nor were such secularizin' shenanigans limited to North America: one of the biggest international folk stars of 1963 was Sister Luc-Gabrielle of Belgium, a.k.a. "the Singing Nun" (g retained in translation), who won hearts all over the world with her zany

"SISTER MYSTIC AND BROTHER OUTLAW" TELLIN' IT LIKE IT IS AT THE PASADENA NUCLEAR DISARMAMENT RALLY.

habit of taking "Sister Adele" (a guitar) for a ride on her Vespa, careening through the Belgian countryside in search of smiling peasant listeners for her next recital.

For their part, *echt* folkies packed up their gunnysacks and headed south to get involved in the civil rights movement. While the likes of the Kingston Trio, Limeliters, and Smothers Brothers appeared weekly on ABC-TV's folxploitation show, Hootenanny, more engaged folkniks, led by Dylan, Baez, Pete Seeger, and Tom Rush, were turning up at sit-ins and marches, often getting hauled off to jail with the rest of their black brothers and sisters, the ultimate validation of the folkie experience. Idealistic youths from all over the country began to drop out of college and do their part, which sometimes meant bunking in sharecroppers' shacks and helping out in the fields. It also meant getting firehosed and hit on the head. White southerners just didn't cotton to their type. Robert Shelton, Imperial Wizard of the Ku Klux Klan, put it this way: "Some of the whites that I witnessed participating in this civil rights struggle—these sex perverts and beatniks and pinkos, tennis-shoe wearers and all—are in all probability perverts just as oddball as some nigras." (As racist epithets went, "tennis-shoe wearer" ranked up there with "carpetbagger" and "communist"—though one can't help but feel they'd have preferred "Fred Braun sandal-wearer," if only they had known). Thus bitten by chiggers, sweaty and reeking, roughed up and rolled in the clink, folkies were at last experiencing firsthand the stuff of which the Blues are made.

By 1965, Dylan had come a long way from his early days as the aw-shucksin', Freewheelin' Bob. He'd become Byronic Bob: the ultimate poet/prophet/sage of the Sixties, the Philosopher King of the folkies. His transformation from ramblin' boy to Messiah was complete at the 1963 Newport Folk Festival, when, one by one, the pillars of the folk establishment—Baez, Pete Seeger, Theo Bikel, Peter, Paul and Mary—mounted the stage in a reverent trance to join Bob for a show-stopping, hallelujah chorus of "Blowin' in the Wind."

Of course, all this meant big cross-over popularity, too, and Bob was teetering dangerously on the brink of commercialism. The engineer's cap and Iron Boy overalls were gone, traded in for a leather jacket, Rayban sunglasses, and pointy-toed Beatle boots. Folkies got a taste of things to come (though they hoped, prayed that it was but a phase) with the album Highway 61 Revisited, wherein Dylan had dropped his honest acoustic to play electric. And as he made the shift, teenyboppers began to take notice. Teen magazine advised its readers on what to expect from "A Dream Date with Bob Dylan":

> If you had a date with Bob, he would take you in your poor boy shell and bellbottoms to some joint for a bite to eat. No fancy dinners or lavish restaurants. Then you and the gang would follow him along to some Greenwich Village coffeehouse....After the show ends and you and the crowd have had another snack at another joint, all of you go to his pad for a bull session until dawn. That's what Dylan digs—a hazy dark room with a group of people just talking.

Most folkies chose to interpret all this as just so much playful, enigmatic Bobism. They were in for a shock, then, at the 1965 Newport Folk Festival, where Dylan singlefootedly booted purists back to the precious obscurity from whence they came. Electric bluesman Michael Bloomfield, then part of Dylan's backup group, remembers that fatal performance:

> Dylan wore rock and roll clothes....He looked like something from West Side Story....We finished with 'Like a Rolling Stone,' Dylan's hit single. I thought we were winning the crowd over. I thought we were boffo, smasheroo. After it was over, I said, 'Bob, how do you think we did?' And he said, 'They were booing. Didn't you hear it?' I said, 'No, man. I thought it was cheers.' Then Peter Yarrow from Peter, Paul and Mary came out and said, 'Well, come on, let's hear it for Bob.' And all he heard was 'Booo! Booo!' He was up there pleading for about ten minutes, and then in the back room he said, 'Oh, Bob, go out and do one of your old numbers. Come on, Bob, you don't want to let your fans down.'
>
> In penance—in penance!—Dylan put on his old Martin and played. But he sang, 'It's All Over Now, Baby Blue.' You know, 'The sky is falling down on you, It's all over now, Baby Blue.'

All over but for a new, eminently commercial hybrid called "Folk Rock"—launched that day in Newport, and adopted by everyone from the Byrds to Donovan to Sonny and Cher. This pair was, perhaps, the most apt embodiment of the new medium's general level of integrity: a tone-deaf Romeo and Juliet who chugged along for a few lame hits before sinking into television. Dylan himself pitched in with a few songs written to order for the winsome pair. And with that, the old folkies truly were laid out in graves dug "long and narrow"—set a-spinnin' there by Cher's occasional bits of post-folk wisdom:

"I think there has been just too much protesting. Maybe there are a lot of problems in the world, but it seems like an okay place to me!"

Archive Photos

The Beatles

We were driving through Colorado and we had the radio on and eight of the Top Ten songs were Beatles songs. In Colorado!

"They were doing things nobody was doing. Their chords were outrageous, just outrageous, and their harmonies made it all valid....But I kept it to myself that I really dug them. Everybody else thought they were for the teenyboppers, that they were gonna pass right away....[But] I knew they were pointing the direction where music had to go...in my head, the Beatles were it.
—Bob Dylan, 1971

In [the early] days, when the Beatles were depressed, we had this little chant. I would yell out, 'Where are we going, fellows?' They would say, 'To the top, Johnny!'....And I would say, 'Where is that, fellows?' And they would say, 'To the toppermost of the poppermost!'
— John Lennon, 1980

By the early Sixties, pop music had gotten awfully dull. The Number One song of 1963 was "Sugar Shack," by a fellow named Jimmy Gilmer, upon whom posterity frowns. About the most exciting thing that had happened to American rock so far in the decade was surfing music. This helps to explain the popularity of folk: in such a hothouse of tedium, one finds the wherewithal to sprout a social conscience and sing about it. And Elvis? Whither goest our faded King? The King was withering in Hollywood, recycling the same dumb movie over and over again, a lacquered robot.

Meanwhile, in the squalid town of Liverpool, a boom was on. Inspired by the first American rock revolution of 1956— Elvis, Little Richard, Chuck Berry, Buddy Holly, and the basic R&B sound that served as the bedrock of it all—"teddy boy" club bands were turning away from traditional ("trad") and skiffle-type music to play rock and roll. But the Liverpool craze was spreading too fast—there weren't enough clubs to play in, and what clubs there were often restricted the

playing of rock and roll. Hence the proving ground became Hamburg, where Liverpool "Merseybeat" bands played frantic all-night gigs: "loud and fast and raw," wrote Lester Bangs, "...hour after hour, using stimulants to maintain the pace, forcing members who had thought they could not sing to take the mike when the leader's lungs gave out." A dissonant, exciting sound came out of this, all crashing drums and "yeah-yeah-yeah" and rhythm guitar, and it was mostly trash. Exciting trash, though, and a lot of fun.

Those who made it in Hamburg moved back to Liverpool's "Cavern Club," a seedy basement that had become a favorite teen hangout and the hub of the Merseybeat Sound. The club was about a hundred yards from the office of Brian Epstein, the owner of a record-store chain, who in October 1961 walked over to hear The Beatles, a group which, or so he'd heard, had come to dominate the Liverpool music scene:

"I saw four boys with very little stage presentation," Epstein remembered. "They had scrubby haircuts and scrubby clothes—black jackets and jeans. But I recognized the appeal of their beat and I rather liked their humor. Through it all came a quality of personal presence...that seemed to me to be full of possibilities. I got friendly with them and became their manager."

At the time, the rock-and-roll craze in Liverpool was strictly a subculture, a club thing; commercially, its possibilities were almost nil. Epstein was well aware of this: he booked the Beatles in church halls, cabarets, tiny clubs, and youth centers. He went slowly. Meanwhile, he sent out press releases that claimed, with typical hucksterish hyperbole, that his group "would someday be bigger than Elvis."

"One did everything," he said. "One worked very hard. One shouted from the rooftops about this group when there was no enthusiasm for groups. People thought you were mad, but you went on shouting."

In 1962 the Beatles were polled as the top group in Liverpool. This didn't amount to much. Around that time, they failed an audition with British Decca (an event that Decca executives would recall with damp eyelids in the days and years to come) and signed instead with EMI, which released "Love Me Do" in October. The song peaked at Number 21 on the charts in the United Kingdom. Epstein began to book them in larger ballrooms, theaters, and, finally, concert halls. They caused a sensation in Manchester when they appeared, a month after the release of "Love Me Do," on Granada TV's "Peoples and Places." By the time "Please Please Me" hit Number One in February 1963, the first rumblings of Beatlemania were felt about Britain. Then, abruptly, the earth split open and everyone dove in: the Beatles' first album stayed at Number One for thirty consecutive weeks, replaced by their second album, *With the Beatles,* for the next twenty-two.

In America, a state of blissful calm and bad music reigned. "Please Please Me" failed to make the charts. "From Me to You" hit its peak at 116, forty notches below that of Del Shannon's version of the same tune, released two months earlier. Introducing the Beatles, the first North American album, went nowhere. The American market, clogged with domestic dregs, was safely sealed off to foreign intrusion.

One day in the summer of 1963, while changing planes in London, Ed Sullivan and his wife were greeted by a bizarre sight: swarms of young people, thousands of them, holding banners which read (cryptically enough) WE LOVE YOU, RINGO, HI, JOHN, HELLO, PAUL, WE LOVE YOU, BEATLES. "Naturally his curiosity was aroused," promoter Sid Bernstein remembers, "and he asked the airplane attendants, 'What are the Beatles?' He thought it was an animal act. They told him the Beatles were a group of musicians from Liverpool who were arriving at the airport within the next hour, and that these were their fans, out in force to meet the plane. Sullivan decided he had to be the first in America to put them on television."

"I made up my mind that this was the same sort of mass hit hysteria that had characterized the Elvis Presley days," Sullivan would later recall.

"So this is America," said Ringo, deadpan, disembarking at Kennedy Airport. "They all seem out of their minds."

By the time the Beatles arrived in New York in February 1964, Capitol Records had sold over two and a half million copies of "I Want to Hold Your Hand." The "mass hit hysteria" of British Beatlemania had finally crossed over. Three months before, the Beatles had brought the house down, almost literally, at the London Palladium, followed a few weeks later by a much-touted Royal Command Performance attended by Princess Margaret and the queen mother. The New York Times picked up the story in December ("Britons succumb to 'Beatlemania'"). That was followed in January by an eight-page, seventeen-picture account in Life magazine: "Four Screaming Mopheads Break Up England: Here Come Those Beatles." And finally, perhaps the most potent affirmation of all, Bob Hope appeared on North American television wearing a Beatles wig.

Capitol's publicity campaign was relentless: a million copies of a four-page tabloid on the Beatles were distributed to deejays, retail outlets, and the press, as was a seven-inch (17.5 cm) long-playing record containing three songs and an "open-ended interview with the Beatles"—that is, a segment of pre-recorded "answers" by John, Paul, George, and Ringo so that North American deejays could pretend to hold personal interviews with the group ("I say, John," a newly-Anglicized deejay might ask, "many parents seem not to fancy you lads. Any thoughts?" "It is to larf, mate…"). In New York, deejays vied for "Fifth Beatle" status, conspiring to corner the group on arrival, and thus to become the Beatles' own Beatrice, their savvy guide to the States. Meanwhile, they assured listeners that the real inside dope on the Fab Four was available only on WINS/WABC/WMCA, each of whom made it abundantly clear where youngsters could go to greet the group.

"The scene [at Kennedy Airport]," Tom Wolfe wrote, "was the expected madhouse, 4,000 kids ricocheting all over the place, hurling themselves at plate glass to try to break through into the customs area when the Beatles got off the plane and came through, things like that."

Two nights later, on February 9, 1964, the second rock-and-roll revolution began. Music critic Greil Marcus, who was

THE MOPTOPS "RELAX"
BY ENGAGING IN TYPI-
CALLY CHEEKY ANTICS
AT THEIR HOLLYWOOD
HILLS HIDEOUT DUR-
ING AN AMERICAN
CONCERT TOUR,
AUGUST 1964.

a college student in California at the time, remembers:

> There had been an item in the paper that day about a British rock and roll group which was to appear on The Ed Sullivan Show that night: "The Beatles" (A photo too—were those wigs, or what?). I was curious—I didn't know they had rock and roll in England—so I went down to a commons room where there was a TV set, expecting an argument from whoever was there about which channel to watch.
>
> Four hundred people sat transfixed as the Beatles sang 'I Want to Hold Your Hand,' and when the song was over the crowd exploded. People looked at the faces (and the hair) of John, Paul, George, and Ringo and said Yes (and who could have predicted that a few extra inches of hair would suddenly seem so right, so necessary?)...Back at the radio I caught 'I Saw Her Standing There' and was instantly convinced it was the most exciting rock and roll I'd ever heard....The next weeks went by in a blur. People began to grow their hair....A friend got his hands on a British Beatles album unavailable in the U.S. and made a considerable amount of money charging people for the chance to hear John Lennon sing 'Money (That's What I Want)'—at two bucks a shot. Excitement wasn't in the air; it was the air.

The Beatles' visit to America lasted just over a week, and left the country in a collective swoon. Brits delighted in gaudy accounts of the Fab Four's absolute conquest of the Yanks. Though the group might have barnstormed the country, playing one-night stands in all the major cities, they made only two concert appearances besides the Sullivan Show—at Carnegie Hall (Epstein thought his boys weren't quite ready for 18,000-seat Madison Square Garden) and the Coliseum in Washington, D.C. The pandemonium at Carnegie was such that pedestrians throughout midtown Manhattan thought a riot had broken out in the vicinity of Fifty-Seventh Street.

The rest of 1964 went by in a blur of Beatlemania. In April, the Beatles filled all top five positions on Billboard's singles charts. Meet the Beatles, Capitol's version of the United Kingdom release, With the Beatles, became the best-selling record in history up to that time. Clinging giddily to the Beatles' coattails, all sorts of mediocre "Merseybeat" bands flooded the American market (some of them, such as Gerry and the Pacemakers, also managed by the wily Epstein), transforming the North American music scene along with the youth culture it reflected. In the wake of the British Invasion, folk-music coffeehouses folded one after the other, or else yielded to the wave of the future, their once-pensive patrons dancing to Beatles tunes and calling each other "luv" and "mate." Beatles' wigs were not bought merely as novelties—they were worn, by the millions. The Beatle's first movie, A Hard Day's Night, opened to extraordinary popular and critical acclaim. Finally, when Ringo entered the hospital in December to have his tonsils out, candlelight vigils were held all over the world.

Pedants agreed that the Beatles phenomenon was "an ideal subject for a sociological study of the dynamics of fads and crazes and of social stratification." Scholarly papers were churned out by the dozens in a manic rush to make the journals before the fad passed away. The New York Times ran a front-page story, PEOPLEWISE BEATLES PROVIDE NEW STUDY FOR SOCIOLOGISTS, summarizing some of the general conclusions:

> The Beatles serve as symbols of:
> • Adolescent revolt against parental authority.
> • Status that comes from belonging to a group, in this case, of other Beatlemaniacs.
> • Sex, both from the supposed erotic nature of the Beatles' music and the way they perform it and from the appeal they seem to have to the 'mother instinct.'
> • Success by persons who are seen as fellow teenagers (although none of the Beatles are under 21) and as underdogs who came from the wrong side of the tracks and made good.

© FPG International

HEY-HEY FOR THE
MONKEES! THE
NUMBER-ONE BEA-
TLES RIP-OFF GROUP.

• The frenetically felt urgency for having a good time and living life fast in an uncertain world plagued with mortal dangers.

Confronted with such portentous analyses, a "typical Beatles fan" ("female, in her early teens," noted the Times) grimaced ecstatically and squealed: "They're so keeee-oooot!"

For the next few years, it was a Beatles World. When John Lennon proclaimed in August 1966 that "[The Beatles are] more popular than Jesus," he was, however tactlessly, engaging in understatement. In what was, after all, a highly secularized world, the Beatles had precipitated an unprecedented "pop explosion," a phenomenon which Greil Marcus defined as:

> ...an irresistible cultural explosion that cuts across lines of class and race...and, most crucially, divides society itself by age.... Pop explosions must link up with, and accelerate, broad shifts in sexual behavior, economic aspirations, and political beliefs.... [At] its heart, a pop explosion attaches the individual to a group—the fan to an audience, the solitary to a generation...while at the same time it increases one's ability to

respond to a particular pop artifact...with an intensity that verges on lunacy.

All the other rock bands concocted their various "images" in relation to the Beatles: the Rolling Stones, the Kinks, and the Who stayed deliberately to the "left" of the moptops, serving as "bad boy" counterparts; lesser lights such as Herman's Hermits, the Dave Clark Five, the Searchers, Peter and Gordon, et al, fecklessly imitated them. Rockers who fancied themselves "progressive" pretended to "pick up where the Beatles left off." Rip-off bands abounded: there were the "Beetles," "Beatlerama," "Beatle Buddies" (a female version of the group), "Beattle [sic] Mash," and so on; in Czechoslovakia alone, there were more than 500 quartets with Beatles-like names. The most notable American rip-off, The Monkees, became so popular that there were even Monkees rip-offs.

The Beatles' influence touched not only the music but every aspect of popular culture, including hair, clothes, and speech—the more Beatles-like, the more "in." Even the movies were Beatlized: jump-cut editing and fast-motion effects, stock gimmicks of many a cheesy Sixties movie, were largely derived from A Hard Day's Night and Help! (the Beatles' second movie). And then, of course, there was the commercial side of it all: in 1965 alone, over $50 million worth of Beatles books, buttons, t-shirts, posters, scarves, and wallets were sold in the United States. Worldwide record sales were almost too staggering to tabulate; in order to gauge the whole effect, one might also take into account the sales generated by rip-off groups, as well as (why not?) those of all groups and various cultural detriti that had in some way sprung from the Beatles. In October 1965 a grateful Queen Elizabeth made each Beatle an honored Member of the British Empire, in recognition of the Beatle Industry's revitalizing impact on the British economy (to say nothing of the country's dreary pre-Beatles image).

Artistically, too, the Beatles were growing. What had separated their earlier music from that of its imitators, critics averred, was its "melodic quality," which stood on its own apart from the characteristic rock beat—though the lyrics tended to be the standard teen-romance stuff. But as for their new stuff (ca. 1965 on), far from the old "yeah-yeah-yeah-she-loves-you-love-me-do-hoo," the words now offered "penetrating insights" into the human condition, as in such songs as "Eleanor Rigby" (life is dull, people are lonely) or "Nowhere Man" (people are confused, lonely), or even such inscrutable tracks as "I Am the Walrus" (John claims to be "the walrus," though is really only "the eggman"; Paul, we later learn, in another song, is "the walrus"). Clearly, it was no longer a matter of simply being "keee-ooot." People at all levels of society, from writers and artists to academicians and bankers, regarded the Beatles as latter-day Magi.

No wonder, then, that in late 1966 the world was plunged into chaotic uncertainty amid rumors that the band was breaking up. Their last-ever live performance, they had vowed, was an August concert in San Francisco, whereupon the individual members scattered: George to India, to bone up on playing the sitar; John to make his solo acting debut in How I Won the War; Paul to write movie scores; and Ringo to paint his house. A regular St. Vitus' dance of dismayed fans swarmed over Brian Epstein's lawn in protest, prompting Epstein to call a press conference: the Beatles, he assured us, would soon be back in the studio to engage in an historic project, the album to end all albums, a Statement....

The next six months were all fierce speculation. In February a single was released, "Penny Lane"/"Strawberry Fields Forever," the B-side an apparent discourse on worldly illusion and the Veil of Maya—knocking the hippies flat, their minds blown and smoldering. Then in spring some tapes leaked out. For a few weeks a song-in-progress called "A Day in the Life Of" was played on the radio, then quickly withdrawn. Beatles scholars diverted themselves with the gleaning of its symbols ("'Four thousand holes in Blackburn, Lancashire'?...'Four thou—'...needle marks?—!—Oh, wowww—"). All the while the Beatles plugged away in the studio, spending an alleged 700 hours (their first album had taken twelve) to record layer upon layer of special effects, to dub in huge orchestras, one hundred-voice choirs, sitars,

thirteen-kilocycle whistles (which, hey man, humans can't hear—but it *freaks out dogs!*).

Then came the announcement: on Sunday, June 2, 1967, at midnight, the record would be released for airplay. Any station playing the record even a minute before would find all pre-release privileges forever withheld. Never mind that most stations went off the air at midnight Sunday to service their transmitters—that was the whole point. It was a challenge. The making of history is fraught with such sacrifices. As Langdon Winner wrote in 1968:

> The closest Western Civilization has come to unity since the Congress of Vienna in 1815 was the week the Sgt. Pepper album was released. In every city in Europe and America the stereo systems and the radio played 'What would you think if I sang out of tune...Woke up, got out of bed...looked much older, and the bag across her shoulder...in the sky with diamonds, Lucy in the...' and everyone listened. At the time I happened to be driving across the country on Interstate 80. In each city where I stopped for gas or food...the melodies wafted in from some far-off transistor radio or portable hi-fi. It was the most amazing thing I've ever heard. For a brief while the irreparably fragmented consciousness of the West was unified, at least in the minds of the young.

No less than The Partisan Review declared the Sgt. Pepper album "an astounding accomplishment for which no one could have been wholly prepared...gestations of genius that have now come to fruition." Kenneth Tynan thought it a milestone in the history of western civilization; The New York Review of Books proclaimed "a new and golden Renaissance of song"; and Newsweek drew parallels between the Beatles and T. S. Eliot. A few weeks after the Sgt. Pepper release, the Beatles kicked off the Summer of Love by singing "All You Need Is Love" to over 200 million viewers via satellite. This, then, was the apotheosis of the wacky Beatlemania craze that had swept

IS PAUL DEAD? THE
ALBUM COVERS FOR
ABBEY ROAD AND *MAG-*
ICAL MYSTERY TOUR
CARRY SINISTER
SUBLIMINAL
CONNOTATIONS.

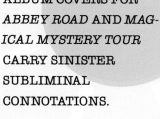

Britain four years earlier: from pudgy, koala-cute madcaps, the Beatles had evolved into four shaggy saints, with their lank hair, mustaches, granny glasses, and ascetic cheekbones. Where could they go from there? *Dowwwn.*

In August 1967, Brian Epstein died of a pill overdose. The Beatles got the news while on retreat with their new guru, the slaphappy Maharishi Mahesh Yogi. The group announced that thenceforth they would manage themselves, and thus proceeded to write, cast, direct, and edit a television movie, Magical Mystery Tour, a silly slice of psychedelic baloney that flopped so badly that much of the impact of Sgt. Pepper was vitiated in one stroke. Dismayed, the Beatles donned kurta sandals and tunics and took off with the Maharishi for Rishikesh-above-the-Ganges, to chant, fast, and pray along with the likes of Mick Jagger, Mia Farrow, Donovan, and Mike Love of the Beach Boys. The press staked out the ashram to monitor the moptops' spiritual progress; word got out that the Beatles were holding a contest to see who could meditate the longest (Paul triumphed—four straight hours). But Ringo found he didn't like the food, and left early.

Ringo's defection was the first dark inkling of disaster, soon to be embodied by John's new girlfriend, Yoko Ono, the latest aspirant to Fifth Beatle status. Yoko became a Sphinx-like fixture in the recording studio, so annoying that Paul, George, and Ringo could hardly stand to be in the same room with her, much less play music together. The press, in its turn, pounced on Yoko with Nippophobic zeal, denouncing her as a disruptive influence on the group's "harmonic balance." Defiant, John formed the ad-hoc "Plastic Ono Band," incorporating Yoko's wounded-bullock vocals on the album that followed.

Beatles' albums proper, post-Sgt. Pepper, were basically solo efforts. As Anthony Fawcett recalls: "On both the 'White Album' and Abbey Road the close collaboration of the past was gone, and the sessions had turned into Paul with a backing group, John with a backing group, or George with a backing group—there was so much uncertainty and the spirit was broken within the group."

Artistically, too, they were growing apart. George waxed Indian ("Within You, Without You"); John had became more and more politicized ("Revolution," "Give Peace a Chance"); while Paul, for his part, stuck statically to the middle of the road ("Ob-la-di, Ob-la-da," "Maxwell's Silver Hammer") until, in 1969, rumor had it that Paul had died, indeed, several years before. By way of concrete evidence, Detroit deejay Russ Gibbs supplied this food for thought: Paul's enigmatic vocals in "A Day in the Life" have obviously been lifted from some other (earlier?) context, and assimilated, with pointed poignancy, into a song which, after all, celebrates a man who "blew his mind out in a car." And the album covers to Magical Mystery Tour and Abbey Road all but clinch the matter: the first of these, please note, conceals an imposter in a Walrus suit (while the real thing molders in the grave); and, on closer inspection of the Abbey Road cover, one is first startled, then dismayed, to notice that Paul is out-of-step with the others…and barefoot! Obviously, his image has been super-imposed. The three surviving Beatles, Gibbs suggested, were trying to break the news to us symbolically.

There was, however obliquely, some truth to all this: though Paul was alive in the clinical sense, the Beatles, alas, were dead. Anthony Fawcett remembers one of their last meetings as a group:

They all freely admitted that there wasn't enough time on an album for all of them to get their songs on. Paul took the 'military approach,' as he called it—divide the time up into four tracks for John, four for Paul, four for George, and one for Ringo. John said, 'What if I've got more! What if George has more?' [And what if *Ringo* has more?!]…

There was a long pause as each Beatle seemed lost in contemplation. Not wanting to admit that they were becoming individual musicians, Paul spoke slowly, 'When we get in a studio, even on the worst day, I'm still playing bass, Ringo's still drumming, and we're still there, you know.'…

They were all feeling a little hurt. And it was all over.

Rock Festivals

"Nobody leaving the Monterey County Fairgrounds at the end of the Monterey International Pop Festival (June 16 to 18, 1967) could have imagined what a Frankenstein monster they had just helped create," wrote John Morthland in 1975.

Monterey was the site of the first major festival devoted to the celebration of rock and roll as a distinct musical genre and, so far as that went, it was unquestionably the most successful. More than any single event it served to validate rock music in the eyes of its critics, the stern purists of folk and jazz, who thought rock and roll "frivolous," "apolitical," and, of course, "commercial." Of at least one of these dire faults the performers at Monterey were innocent: few of the featured acts, which included Jimi Hendrix, Janis Joplin, Otis Redding, and such San Francisco bands as Jefferson Airplane and the Grateful Dead, had attracted anything more than cult followings prior to their appearances at Monterey. And many of them gave, by their own account, the greatest performances of their careers there, preserved for posterity by D. A. Pennebaker's highly acclaimed documentary, Monterey Pop. The ambience of the event, well organized and attended by responsive, discerning fans, was conducive to such excellence.

So why a "Frankenstein monster"? Because of the times, mostly—after the Monterey Festival in June 1967, life in the swinging Sixties began to lose its charm. The counterculture became a snakepit of drugs and violence, and rock festivals invited almost certain bedlam. With the possible exception of Woodstock (whose musical contribution was irrelevant), Monterey set a standard that would not be equalled. But we're getting ahead of ourselves.

Monterey itself began as a taintedly "commercial" venture, its original promoters hoping to recruit diverse but well-known acts and turn a sizable profit. Cultural impact was, at best, a secondary concern. But others in the rock-and-roll establishment, sick to death of pious folkies disparaging the "purity" of their product, saw the opportunity of a rock festival in loftier terms. Lou Adler, then manager of the Mamas and Papas, remembers his thoughts on being approached by the festival's promoters:

Coincidentally, just a few months before...at a gathering at Cass Eliot's house, someone— I think it was Paul McCartney—said that it was about time that rock and roll became recognized as an art form, instead of a musical phase. Rock and roll had in fact grown up; we had experienced the Beatles and the Rolling Stones, and Dylan going electric. By the time...I met again with the promoters and other artists, those three days at Monterey seemed like a great idea—it could be a celebration, a festival, that would show the evolution of contemporary music, and demonstrate where it might be heading.

Adler and other enthusiasts decided the festival should be nonprofit, with all proceeds going to charity.

The promoters weren't geared to that thinking," as Adler mildly put it, so a group of backers, including Adler, Paul Simon, and John Phillips, bought the dates and proceeded to organize the festival themselves. They set up a "board of governors" comprised of such rock luminaries as Mick Jagger, Paul McCartney, and Andrew Oldham (manager of the Rolling Stones) to help select the talent and moreover persuade the talent to accept expenses only for their performances. The industry rallied around with free ads in both Billboard and Cash Box, and future television rights were sold to ABC (which declined Pennebaker's film on the grounds that the Jimi Hendrix scenes were too suggestive). Finally they settled on a theme, "Music, Love, and Flowers," which piqued the curiosity of local authorities, who responded by assigning hundreds of policemen to watch over the expected "hippie invasion."

In all, some 50,000 of the exasperating longhairs showed up (capacity at the fairgrounds was 7,100), many of whom opted not to pay and do their bit for charity. But despite deadbeats and the crush of the crowd, it turned out to be a golden occasion for hippies and performers alike, a proper inauguration for the Summer of Love: Diggers from

the Haight distributed dope and granola; volunteer doctors dealt ably with the freak-outs; and interesting cultural exhibits were available throughout the fairgrounds. Janis Joplin, Jimi Hendrix, and Otis Redding gave performances that launched them into stardom (and later legend-dom, as all three would be gone within a few years).

"Every performer said he or she felt as if he or she were getting a performance in return from the audience," Adler remembers. "It was magical, and it became a total environment. The festival had become the town, and the town had become the festival. I wasn't exactly sure what had worked, but from the time I saw the police putting flowers in their helmets, I knew that something had."

That, however, was not the whole story. Though more than $200,000 had been netted for charity—for ghetto music programs and free clinics—venal bookkeepers absconded with most of the funds. As for the police, floral-hatted or not, they professed to be shocked by the wide-spread drug abuse and public sex. It was all too much of a hassle: though conceived as an annual event, the festival never returned to Monterey.

But Monterey was not remembered for its sorry after-math, but rather for its great music, lurid images (such as Hendrix setting fire to his guitar), and huge, mostly paying, crowds. Inspired, dubious promoters staged a number of lesser rock festivals throughout 1968. These travesties followed a pattern of sorts: amid remote rural squalor, thousands of duped spectators would sit gloomy and stoned, waiting for acts that had been promised but never signed, listening to whomever appeared instead on substandard sound systems. This made people mad.

"Be prepared for a bummer this summer," Rolling Stone warned its readers in 1969, in reference to the increasing incidence of violence at rock festivals.

Larger and larger crowds were attending the festivals. However, they were not the gentle, free-lovin' hippies of two years before, but rather what many of these same people had in the meantime become: militant radical "freaks," as they now preferred to call themselves, whose dreams of peace and a better world had died with the Summer of Love, with the assassinations of Martin Luther King and Robert F. Kennedy, with the ongoing carnage in Vietnam, and with the election of Nixon. The festivals became a kind of last refuge for tripping malcontents to come together and let it all hang out—that is, to scream at the pigs and stomp each other amid gunfire and bursting tear-gas shells. As many came with no intention of paying ("The music belongs to the people, man!"), rumbles between gatecrashers and cops effectively ended some festivals before they'd begun.

Incessant riots broke out at an Easter-week festival in Palm Springs, ending with two people shot and 250 arrested. The Newport '69 festival was an even bigger disaster: 300 injured, 75 arrested, and over $50,000 in property damage. Though its promoters grossed over $1 million, they still ended up with a deficit of $150,000. A subsequent festival in Denver closed in a fog of tear gas, with thousands staggering away from the scene, audience and performers alike, screaming and retching.

One key to the success of the Woodstock Music and Art Fair in August 1969 was that police agreed not to show up. Embittered by the all-too-popular "pig" appellation, the police consensus as far as these "freak-fests" went was, in effect, To hell with it: Let 'em strand themselves in the boonies, run wild, and die. So much the better. But at Woodstock, in the very absence of authority, with hardly a trace of the hated Establishment, and despite what proved to be perhaps the most appalling conditions yet (constant rain, a world of mud, overflowing toilets, and food and water shortages) the kids behaved pretty well.

In lieu of the fuzz, organizers recruited one hundred members of the Hog Farm Commune in Santa Fe, New Mexico, flying them up to New York in a specially chartered jet. Hog Farmers were reputed to be among the last of the old-style hippies: benign, humorous, and too stoned to bother with Eastern-mystical pretensions—just a bunch of farmers. Their emblem, worn proudly on the sleeves of their denim jackets, was an angelic pig perched atop a guitar fret. Thus grubby and bemused, with broods of flower-tykes in

tow, the Hog Farmers arrived at Kennedy Airport to meet the press. Hugh Romney (a.k.a. "Wavy Gravy"), one of the commune's leaders, remembers the brief conference that followed:

"When we got off the plane in New York City to go to Woodstock, we found a lot of reporters who asked, 'What are you going to do for security?' And we suddenly realized that we weren't there just for cutting the trails. I said, 'Do you feel secure?' A reporter said, 'Yeah,' so I said, 'It seems to be working.' He said, 'Well, what are you going to use?' And I said, 'Custard pies and seltzer bottles.'"

The festival had been forced out of its original site near Woodstock, settling instead on Max Yasgur's 600-acre (240 ha) farm at White Lake, New York. Amid the milling Guernseys (Hog Farmers posted signs: DON'T BOTHER MAX'S COWS. LET THEM MOO IN PEACE.), a ramshackle city formed overnight—tens of thousands of tents, campers, and make-shift shacks. Cars coming from all directions were backed up bumper to bumper for thirty miles (48 km), most of them eventually abandoned, as a staggering number of pilgrims, nearly half a million in all, poured into the pastures of Yasgur's Farm.

The music came across as little more than a distant rumble. Most people were unable to see, much less hear, the acts, perhaps the greatest lineup of rock talent ever assembled onstage: The Who, Buffalo Springfield, Crosby Stills and Nash, The Band, Joe Cocker, Janis Joplin, Jimi Hendrix, and so on. But the music was only one aspect of the total experience, which had become a glorious symbol of youth solidarity: the Woodstock Nation, living out the lost, Edenic ideals of the "love generation," romping in the mud, skinny-dipping, sharing tents, food, and dope. If only for a few days, the world of cops, tear gas, Nixon, and napalm seemed far away.

When Woodstock was over, It was over: the Nation dispersed, and the garden was closed.

© Wide World Photos

ALTAMONT, ONE OF
THE TRULY GREAT
BUMMERS OF THE
ROCK ERA. ABOVE:
MICK JAGGER SINGS
WHILE THE SECURITY-
MINDED HELL'S
ANGELS STOMP
ANOTHER SPECTATOR.

At the end of a highly successful North American concert tour, the Rolling Stones decided to thank their fans by holding a free concert in December 1969.

"Woodstock hung in the air like a rainbow," Robert Christgau wrote. "It seemed only fitting to climax all that long-haired pomp and circumstance with yet another celebration of communal freeness."

But things went awry from the start. With less than twenty-four hours notice, the site was changed to Altamont Speedway, about forty miles (64 km) southeast of San Francisco. Because of this, such basic necessities as toilets,

food, and water were in short supply, and the sound system broke down repeatedly throughout the day. Still, more than 300,000 showed up, amidst a gathering stench of urine, feces, a lot of vomit (from all the bad drugs going around), and intermittent fires.

As with Woodstock, the police were conspicuously absent. Unlike Woodstock, there were no gentle Hog Farmers to keep the peace. That job had been awarded to the Hell's Angels motorcycle club: they came cheap ($500 worth of beer), were countercultural heroes of a sort ("our outlaw brothers," the hippies called them), and were more in keeping with the Stones' image, which had evolved from "bad-boy" to quasi-Satanic, with Mick Jagger strutting in a cape, calling himself "Lucifer," and singing "Sympathy for the Devil."

The Angels took their job seriously, keeping the audience at bay with weighted poolcues. More and more common as the day wore on was the sight of beaten concertgoers straggling through the crowd, their faces black with dried blood, too stoned to know what had hit them. Nor were musicians exempt: when Marty Balin of Jefferson Airplane objected, some Angels clambered onstage and beat him senseless. Greil Marcus wrote:

> Every few minutes the music was broken up by waves of terrified screams from the crowd; wild ululations that went on for 30, 40 seconds at a time....All day long people had speculated on who would be killed, on when the killing would take place....A certain inevitability had settled over the event. The crowd had been ugly, selfish, territorialist, throughout the day. People held their space. They made no room for anyone....It was a gray day, and the California hills were bare, cold and dead.

In all, four people died at Altamont: three overdosed and one was murdered. The killing took place at around eight in the evening: with Mick Jagger whirling his cape only a few yards away, the Angels stomped and stabbed to death a young black man named Meredith Hunter. The story goes that they were enraged by Hunter's being with a white woman. And on that note the Sixties drew to a close.

VOLUNTEERS FROM THE HOG FARM COMMUNE CLEAN UP TRASH LEFT BY 300,000 SPECTATORS AT WOODSTOCK.

CHAPTER FOUR

LIFESTYLES

LIFESTYLES

The Pill, Playboys, and Party Girls: A Decade of Fun Begins

For most of the western world, the Sixties began on a note of happy expectancy. Baby-boomers who had grown up during the conservative Fifties ("conservative," though whipped to a gradual froth by such quasi-rebels as Elvis, Brando, and the Beats) hit their hormonal peak at a point in history when anything seemed possible, when there really was money and time enough to be as wackily experimental as they wanted. The Fifties had served to make the middle class feel good about itself again, but it may have been too much of a good thing, too much static suburban serenity, too much of placid old Ike. Kennedy spoke of the need to pass the torch to a new generation, and even Nixon conceded that it was time for a change. In point of fact, there wasn't much difference between the two candidates, either in age or rhetoric, save that one resembled an unshaven Bela Lugosi on television. Hence the image-conscious, youth-obsessed Sixties were ushered in under the heartening banner of Camelot.

Eisenhower was still in office, though, when what is now perceived as the "Sixties Era" got underway—which is not to say on New Year's Day, 1960, but rather on May 9, when the FDA allowed public sale of the first birth-control pill, Enovoid. Tested for years on thousands of Puerto Rican women with unprecedented success, "the pill" became a byword of modernity to swinging men and women throughout the affluent West, who were eager to test the limits of the new sexual freedom. Its influence can hardly be overstated: in 1960, only an estimated 20 percent of American college women had had their first sexual experience; within six years that number had more than tripled, and one out of five women of child-rearing age had a prescription for the pill.

But it wasn't as simple as all that. Pope Paul VI banned the use of the pill—and all artificial birth control—despite its potential to alleviate a worsening population explosion. Moreover, for many "nice girls" of the mainstream middle class, there still was a considerable stigma attached to the idea of being "sexually active." As writer Nora Ephron recalls of her own initiation in the early sixties:

> When I first started with the pill, I would stop taking them every time I broke up with someone. I had a problem making a commitment to sex; I guess it was a hangover from the whole fifties virgin thing....It was impossible for me to think that I might be a person who 'had sex,' so whenever I had no boyfriend it was always a terrible emotional mess. I couldn't start sleeping with someone until I could begin the pill's cycle again. It was awful. Finally, my new gynecologist explained it all to me: 'Dahlink, who knows what's coming around the corner?'

Much of the stigma of female sexual activity was lifted in 1962 with the publication of Helen Gurley Brown's Sex and the Single Girl, the title of which alone struck many people as awesomely iconoclastic, suggesting so bluntly that women could enjoy sex outside of marriage as a routine matter; yes, for the simple (gasp!) fun of it. And these were certainly "nice girls" whom Ms. Brown was addressing— "mouseburgers" she called them, who, by following a few simple precepts, could break free of their prim, nerdy pasts and become bewitching ideals to menfolk in search of a certain *je ne sais quoi* as well as the other thing. "Far from being a creature to be pitied and patronized." Ms. Brown proclaimed, "the single girl is emerging as the newest glamor girl of our times."

And all it took was a little self-assertion! Well, maybe not just a little; in fact, it appeared that nothing less than a complete overhaul of possessions and personality would do—as

GIRLS GET SET TO LIVE LIFE A GO-GO AS THE SIXTIES SWING UNDERWAY.

Ms. Brown put it, one had to "work like a son of a bitch" to become perkily appealing to men. "Ride a Vespa!" she ordered. "Have a memorable beach hat or two....Paint your car hot orange or shocking pink." And if the efficacy of such advice was in doubt, Ms. Brown offered herself as a shining example of mouseburger-makes-good, regaling readers with details of her unfortunate youth in rural Arkansas: "[I was] homely, plagued with acne, flat-chested, not brilliant, and at times mean and cranky." Enough already, I'll get the beach hat!

Though one may shrink at the thought of all the grating behavior it engendered, Sex and the Single Girl became a sort of bible to young women of the Sixties, and was published in twenty-three countries and translated into fifteen languages. It was even made into a movie with Natalie Wood and Tony Curtis, a bizarre art-improves-on-life romance in which Ms. Wood played Helen Gurley Brown (or, rather, a fictional character of that name) as a brisk young editrix whose inner *naif* nature wins the heart of a cynical reporter (Mr. Curtis) who, at the outset, is bent on "exposing" her as just another typical "female," despite her self-reliant posturing.

It is, perhaps, safe to assume that the moral of this movie, and hence the book, was that no matter how "independent" a woman made herself out to be, the bottom line—i.e., getting a man—remained the same. That, at any rate, still seemed the way of things in the early Sixties.

To be young, flighty, and boyishly thin was considered the feminine ideal at the beginning of the decade, traits that were embodied to the point of parody by Cockney super-model Lesley Hornby, better known as "Twiggy." Flat-chested and lanky, Twiggy represented more than just a "look" to women of the Sixties; with her dizzy devil-may-care image, the sixteen-year-old dropout served as a constant reminder to women of all ages to strive for sublime vacuity in word and deed (though, in light of Brownian philosophy, such may be construed as mere cover for some secret sorrow). For years Twiggy's likeness seemed as inescapable

THREE FASHIONABLY THIN MODELS SHOW OFF THE LATEST IN ABOVE-THE-KNEE DRESSES.

as death and taxes—almost as if one were being pursued by the exasperating little sprite: there she was, sprinting, jumping, frugging, at all times deliriously on the go. "Skillions!" she geysered, when asked how much money she made. "Completely disarming and charming," Diana Vreeland remarked of the twitty skillionaire.

With the preeminence of Twiggy, the padded suits, knee-length skirts, and florid hats of the Fifties were relegated to the hopelessly frumpy—replaced by figure-skimming checkerboard dresses, light sleeveless blouses, polka-dotted tights, and low-heeled pumps or sneakers. The last of the serious hats was the pillbox worn by Jackie Kennedy (a formidable fashion idol in her own right, though rather more staid than Twiggy), admired for its chic simplicity. Any

Archive Photos

ready-made designer clothes borrowed much from the styles of the Twenties—that is, the sort of high hemlines and low necklines (disclosing no cleavage if one were ideally bustless) that flappers had danced the Charleston in and that were now, in the madcap Sixties, "making fashion fun again." Quant said of Sixties style:

> There was a time when every girl under twenty yearned to look like an experienced, sophisticated thirty; when round-faced teenagers practiced sucking in their cheeks to achieve interesting hollows; when every girl dreamed of a slinky black dress worn with high heels. All this is in reverse now. Suddenly, every girl with a hope of getting away with it is aiming to look not only under voting age but under the age of consent… Their aim is to look childishly young, naively unsophisticated.

One symptom of all this childish naivete was the popularity of the "bubble" hairdo: a teased, compact spheroid resembling nothing so much as a helmet—the better to play the sometimes rough-and-tumble game of Wily Gamine Gets Her Guy. The bubble was a sassy break from the gelatinous perms of the Fifties, enabling women to gambol about with Twiggy-like insouciance, never having to fret over the collapse of such a bouncy, streamlined bob.

A woman's ability to wax "spontaneous" was that much more enhanced. On a rainy day in the park, say, while one's bewildered (but quite smitten and pipe-smokingly paternal) boyfriend looked on, a bubbleheaded woman might spurn the shelter of the spreading elm to dash with coltish grace amid the puddles, take a few spins on the merry-go-round, and look all the more damply "childish" for her disquieting show of nuttiness.

Helen Gurley Brown, Mary Quant, Twiggy, et al., were all to be thanked for such brave, universalized whimsy.

"What is a Playboy?" asked a 1956 subscription card for Playboy magazine. "Is he simply a wastrel, a ne'er-do-well, a

hat other than the pillbox was worn strictly for conversational purposes, à la Helen Gurley Brown's "memorable beach hat"; finally, after the pillbox had run its course, hats were out, period. After all, one didn't see Twiggy's head covered by anything but her boyish coif of limp yellow hair.

Like Twiggy herself, the scanty new styles of the Sixties emerged from London, which had supplanted Paris as the foremost originator of fashion trends throughout the western world. Mary Quant—who opened her Chelsea boutique Bazaar in 1955 at the age of twenty-one— recognized more than any of her peers the potential to exploit the burgeoning youth market. Her line of cheap, fashionable bum? Far from it: he can be a sharp-minded business executive, a worker in the arts, a university professor, an architect or engineer. He can be many things, providing he possesses a *point of view*. He must see life not as a vale of tears, but as a happy time; he must take joy in his work, without regarding it as the be-all and end-all of living; he must be an alert man, an aware man, a man of taste, a man sensitive to pleasure, a man who—without acquiring the stigma of the voluptuary or dilettante—can live life to the hilt."

Such a man's all-important "point of view" also included, not incidentally, an aptitude for knowing a good pair of bazoongies when he saw them. But then, *that* part of things—that is, the litany of lifestyle imperatives covered by "The Playboy Philosophy"—was more a priority in the repressed Fifties, when full frontal nudity was still something of a novelty, and *Playboy* itself was just another fifty-cent nudie-mag (albeit one that pretended to transcend its genre). With the onset of the permissive, jet-setting, consumerist Sixties, however, single men sought "modern" sophistication in grim earnest, and the pioneering arbiter of this ethos was none other than the suave, agoraphobic editor of *Playboy*, Hugh Hefner.

"I don't have to arrange my life by other people's hours," Hefner declared. "I don't always have to be in some boring conference….I don't even have to shave if I don't feel like it. I don't have to get dressed. I don't have to put on a shirt and tie and suit every day. I just put on a bathrobe!"

Hef summed things up this way: "Our philosophy is that you should work hard and play hard, and strive to get into the sophisticated upper crust."

Never mind the paradox of "striv[ing] to get into the sophisticated upper crust" (or striving to get anywhere, for that matter) while dressed in a bathrobe, the consoling subtext was that if you were a reader of *Playboy,* then, by God, you were already well on your way! You were a connoisseur of the good life: every month you were kept abreast of the latest leisure-oriented perma-press fashions, teak/lime/leather-scented colognes, state-of-the-art audio-

visual technology, and creature comforts of every kind. You were instructed on how to manage the perfect evening *à deux* with such toothsome "continental" recipes as Kahlua Crêpes Bresilienne *(flambé, bien sur)* or any number of fondue sauces or pupu platters. For the playboy of the Sixties was no provincial meat-and-potatoes man; he was a world traveler who not only enjoyed but could pronounce "Crêpes Bresilienne"—preferably while seducing women in such exotic locales as Saint-Tropez and Morocco.

"Jet-setting" accounted for much of the fanciful "playboy mystique." Though passenger-jet travel was still beyond the means of most *Playboy* readers circa 1960, the cut-rate fares that soon came into effect made this dream of playboy glamor a glorious reality: like any globe-trotting *bon vivant,* Joe Average could at last fly about "in shirtsleeves, smoking a pipe, lounging comfortably or even taking a stroll down a long, plush-carpeted cabin, enjoying the soothing strains of a Strauss waltz drifting muted and pleasant from hidden speakers" (as Martin Caiden evoked the experience in his 1959 paean to the jet age, Boeing 707). How better to acquire suave "continental" manners than to go to the source and study them firsthand? And then, of course, every playboy had heard about those foreign chicks, not

Archive Photos

OPPOSITE PAGE: HYPERACTIVE COCK-NEY SUPERMODEL LESLEY "TWIGGY" HORNBY GIDDILY SURVEYS HER NEW LINE OF CLOTHING, LONDON 1967.

BELOW: HUGH HEFNER, THE AGORAPHO-BIC GURU OF SIXTIES "SOPHISTICATION."

HEF AND SOME
BUNNIES HANG OUT
AT THE PLAYBOY CLUB
IN LONDON.

© Wide World Photos

to mention the legendary friskiness of stewardesses (or "stews," as a playboy was wont to say).

Mind, a true playboy was not just a common tourist. So assiduously had he dogged *la dolce vita* that he was now that model of sophistication, "the seasoned traveler"—a personage whom Alitalia Airline's Views to Dine By defined as "[one] who has, at last, graduated from the prerequisite omnibus guide book—who now has time to linger, and enjoy the beauty of the land. No longer does he have a quota of birthplaces, fountains, monuments, churches and museums he must see…He may sit back and 'make like a native' and share with the great the views which have given them respite and moral fortification." For as little as $109 in 1966, playboys could enjoy an entire week of moral fortification on Corfu or Tahiti, at Club Mediterranée, where business quadrupled between 1960 and 1970.

But once a playboy had attained that enviable eyrie, "the sophisticated upper crust," what then? Once he'd become a Citizen of the World in the fullest sense—his "discerning palate" cloyed with innumerable pots of fondue, with serving upon serving of such continentalia as *coq au vin, boeuf bourgignon,* and the gamut of "piquant potables" (though skirting all the while, one hopes, the awful stigma of the "voluptuary")—did he then simply rest on his laurels? Did he withdraw like some wistful, bathrobed Gatsby to the teak-panelled halls of his superfabulous "Playboy Town House,"

with its rich Afghan carpeting, skylight, perpetually roaring hearth, and "Rabbit-escutcheoned" doors?

Not hardly! For the playboy was, above all, a seeker—a Man of Ideas whose outward frippery served only to keep the madding crowd at a distance while he pondered the dictates of his turbulent, questing soul. He cultivated "progressive" political notions. He rejoiced over the broad implications of certain fashion trends, as when bathing suits went topless for a while in 1965 ("When the first topless bathing suits hit the beaches last year," Playboy exulted, "we joined the rest of mankind in hailing the advent of an age of limitless revelation"). Playboys of the vaunted "upper crust" held the world in their hands—women, money, power—but still they probed deeper. They recited poetry, had a learned appreciation for art (though God forbid they should be labelled "dilettantes"), and read such highbrow writers as Nabokov, Bellow, and Styron, right in the pages of their favorite magazine. They were, in short, Renaissance Men.

As sociologists Walter M. Gerson and Sander H. Lund observed in a 1967 Journal of Popular Culture: "[Playboy gives its readers] a goal to achieve, a model of behavior to emulate, and an identity to assume…[that of the] sophisticated, cosmopolitan, urbane, diverse, affluent, intellectual, promiscuous (if that is the word), mature bachelor." And what purpose did such versatility serve? Gerson and Lund explain: "The Playboy becomes multi-dimensional. He can quote Ibsen, Sartre, and Mailer. He is at home at formal dinner parties or hippie beer bashes, and as a consequence he seduces with equal facility sophisticated debutantes and female bohemians." Thus a playboy was one who, no matter how erudite, kept his priorities straight.

And with that let us leave the Playboy with a last glimpse of him as he was, at his best, in the idyllic, liberated Sixties: reclining in his BarcaLounger, smoking a fragrant bowl of Klompen Kloggen tobacco ("Please, may I sniff your Klompen Kloggen?" begs the swooning beauty in the Playboy ad), while his latest lady-love lies curled at his feet, a pair of state-of-the-art stereophonic headphones clamped, or perhaps klomped, to her head.

© H. Wright/FPG International

The Surfer Phenomenon

In "The Pump House Gang," Tom Wolfe relates the poignant story of Donna and her eighteen-year-old boyfriend, "who killed themselves in a murder/suicide pact on the steps of the Pump House. The local explanation was that she couldn't see anything beyond surfing. Her life had come to an end because she was now 21." In fairness to Donna, one should be careful to read "surfing" not only as the insuperable thrill of catching a wave and thereby sitting on top of the world, but also, or rather, as the heady ethos it was—connoting an Endless Summer (though not for Donna) of hanging out at the beach, tanning one's fine young bod a mahogany hue, and finding soulmates of the opposite sex with whom to reflect upon the "Mysterioso" grandeur of the mighty Pacific.

In short, it was a Way of Life—though all too fleeting. Imagine finding that low door in the wall that opened on an Enchanted Beach, knowing all the while that one's banishment to the outside world is inevitable.... Then picture a typical (circa 1960 to 65) Southern California suburban tableau—squat pastel bungalows as far as the eye can see—and our sympathy for Donna may become more than sneaking. *Et in Arcadia ego.*

If you were young and anywhere near a decent beach in the early Sixties, then in all probability, surfing was part of your world. You couldn't get away from it—it dominated every aspect of civilization as you knew it: music, movies, cars, clothes, coiffures. And it didn't matter much whether or not you owned a surfboard (though you probably did); unless you were a total fream (misfit), you went along with it to some extent. If indeed it was your sad lot to be a kook (untalented novice), you compensated by working that much harder on your tan, by bleaching your hair and cheering sportively ("Cowabunga!") for the real hotdogs who were out there taming the wild surf. You wore the requisite baggies, Pendleton shirts, and huarache sandals. You carried your pals and all their gear to oceanside drive-ins in your woodie (station wagon with wooden sides). It was mostly a matter of cultivating the persona. The Beach Boys, after all, numbered but one real surfer among them, Dennis Wilson, while brother Brian—surfing's greatest bard—was actually afraid of the water.

The sport originated in the Hawaiian islands, where Type-A personalities joyously risked being smashed into reefs or simply swallowed whole by the monster waves that pursued them. It had the same intrepid man-against-nature mystique as, say, mountain climbing, though with far nicer amenities: the glittering sand, the warm sun, and of course the buoyant, scantily clad spectators, which helped to assuage the angst-ridden peril of it all. It was high drama and, as such, bound to catch on with self-dramatizing youths the world over: throughout the Pacific Islands, South Africa, Australia, Peru, and especially California, where it was most effectively exploited by American commercialism.

What began in the late Fifties as a fairly isolated fad, based in suburban beach-communities around Los Angeles, boomed into a national craze with the growing popularity of such "surfer bands" as Dick Dale and the Del Tones, the Pyramids, the Challengers, and the Ventures. The "ear-splitting noise called 'surfing music'" (as Life magazine impugned it) was mostly instrumental at first, dominated by the sound of twangy, reverb-charged Stratocaster guitars. Such hits as "Walk Don't Run," "Rebel Rouser," "Wipe Out," "Let's Go Trippin'," and "Ram-Bunk-Shush" captured the frenetic feel of surf 'n' party excitement, the vocals limited to the occasional "hey, yeah!" or "hup-hup-hup! *heigh*-ohhh!" urging surfers to stay atop that wave to the bitter, sprawling end—a terse but suggestive statement that echoed throughout surfing meccas on every continent.

By 1961, there were a number of surfer-oriented radio stations in California that offered not only the music but also daily reports on surfing conditions and a vast lexicon of surfer slang. The Wilson brothers, Brian, Dennis, and Carl, along with their cousin, Mike Love, all of whom hailed from the archetypal suburb of Hawthorne, were ardent listeners of

THE BEACH BOYS, POETS OF THE SURFING ETHOS.

OPPOSITE PAGE, BOTTOM: FRANKIE AND ANNETTE TENSELY CONFRONT SOME NON-SURFERS IN *BEACH BLANKET BINGO*.

KFWB radio, "the surfer's choice." One day the boys got together and made a list of surfer-terms heard on KFWB, out of which they wrote the song, "Surfin'." Calling themselves The Pendletones (in the unrealized hope of getting free Pendleton shirts), they paid to make a demonstration record at a local studio, with Carl Wilson providing the only instrumental backup on "Surfin'" and its flip-side, "Luau."

Despite nasally, off-key vocals and the rather stark strumming of Carl's lone guitar, the record was released on the Candix label and soon hit number one locally and number 75 on the national Hot 100. Hearing their record on the radio for the first time, Brian Wilson celebrated by bleaching his hair; Carl went on a milkshake bender until he threw up.

Renamed the Beach Boys, the group made its first public appearance on New Year's Eve, 1961, at the Municipal Auditorium in Long Beach, California. The Beach Boys stole the show by playing and re-playing their entire repertoire of three songs—songs which invoked, in all their nasal simplicity, the ample philosophy of being young, tan, and on the beach, hangin' ten for the one you love. One needed only to hear the wild, undiscriminating roars of their fellow surfin' suburbanites to know that the Boys had tapped into the *Zeitgeist* in a big way. Other Stratocaster-equipped groups may have set the mood of surfing mania, but the Beach Boys were pioneers in putting it all into its properly poetic context.

Thus, while fellow bandmembers applied themselves to learning their instruments, Brian Wilson spent much of 1962 in conference with his muse, finding terms in which to spread the surfing ideal throughout California and beyond—yea, unto the beachless world of Middle America, where "You don't have to go the the islands to have a lot of fun/Just pretend your patio's an island in the sun." The gist of this message achieved a kind of apotheosis with the Beach Boys' first megahit, "Surfin' USA"—a song which began with the almost surreal premise that, were there but an ocean at everyone's disposal (no matter how sadly landlocked most Americans were), then the surfin' craze would be the greatest democratic phenomenon of all time, with armies of baggie-clad youths stacked thousands to a wave.

In 1963, as blacks marched on Washington and the conflict deepened in Vietnam and John F. Kennedy expressed solidarity with walled-in Berliners, youngsters of the white American middle class were swilling oceans of beer and dreaming of the perfect wave. Escapism was the order of the day, the more mindless, the better. And in that year of wonders, surfing was just the ticket.

Frederick Wardy of Surfer magazine wrote: "Surfing is a release from exploding tensions of twentieth-century living. [It is an] escape from the hustling, bustling city world of steel and concrete, a return to nature's reality."

Hollywood saw the point. With no end of shameless variation on a gleefully idiotic theme, surfer movies were churned out at a blurry rate: Ride The Wild Surf, Surf Crazy, Surf Party, Beach Party, Beach Blanket Bingo, Beach Ball, Bikini Beach, How to Stuff a Wild Bikini, Bikinis on Parade, It's a Bikini World (indeed), and then—in a B-movie genre-clash born of cynical ingenuity—The Ghost in the Invisible Bikini, The Horror of Party Beach, Monster from the Surf, and so on unto a kind of a monster mash wipe-out.

The "plots" of these movies (allegories, really) were based on the myth of the Menaced Paradise: surfin', dancin', guitar-strummin' innocents were typically besieged by such invaders as grumpy greasers, grasping real-estate developers, or martians, zombies, and waxen vampires in need of a good tan. Not to worry, though! The fun is so infectious that even the gnarliest villains are won over in the end, joining the kids for a last rousing rendition of the surfer-stomp as the sun sets and the credits roll.

And then, for surfers who still bothered to read (if for no other reason than the sheer impossibility of lugging a TV or hi-fi onto the beach), there were such inspiring tomes as The Beach Book, by Gloria Steinem (yes, the same) whose dust jacket promised definitive tutorials on "making a kite, a

sandcastle, a bikini…reading palms, rubbing backs, burying friends." Eighty-four pages are devoted to "The Suntan," and Steinem writes with an almost forbidding sense of purpose on the subject of how to develop a beautiful bustline.

A reference to the Sixties as a "Decade of Change" becomes no idle cliché when one considers this book.

The surfing phenomenon crested in 1963 and then crashed rather suddenly, all but washed away by the British Invasion and the more provocative escapism of the hippies. Save for a few ragged packs of party animals strewn about the Southern California coastline (surburban dropouts who left home to live in garages with their fellow beach bums, themselves a kind of early hippie), surfers abruptly faded from the scene in late 1964, trading their "bushy-bushy blond hairdos" for the brunette mop-top wigs of the Fab Four. For eight months no American male group made the top of the singles charts until the Beach Boys hit number one with "I Get Around" on July 4. Surfing pretty much vanished as a subject of pop music. The Beach Boys themselves went vaguely "psychedelic" in 1966 with the album Pet Sounds, which featured multi-track tripping music.

An inglorious coda to the funny, sunny surfin'-music craze was the Monterey International Pop Festival in 1967, which featured such progressive acts as the Byrds, the Who, the Mamas and the Papas, and Janis Joplin. The Beach Boys were invited to headline as the Festival's one surefire commercial draw, but they pulled out at the last moment. "All those people from England who play acid rock," Brian Wilson fretted. "If the audience is coming to see them, they're going to hate us." The Beach Boys were replaced by Otis Redding, whose performance at Monterey elevated him to the status of official "Soul Man to the hippies." Throughout the festival snide references were made to the Beach Boys' absence, as conspicuous as it was unlamented.

The final malediction came from Jimi Hendrix, pausing between licks on his twelve-string, acid-toned Rickenbacker: "You heard the last of surfing music!"

A SURFER GIRL WITH HER BEST FRIENDS.

Swinging London

Consider the miniskirt, and you begin to grasp the essence of the "youthquake" that rumbled throughout the Sixties and seemed to topple so much of the fusty old world order. Designed by Mary Quant, the mini was wildly popular among (as Quant put it) "the daughters of dukes and the daughters of dock workers." That, in so many words, was a development with revolutionary implications: no longer did high fashion evoke a necessary distinction between rich and poor—rather, it differentiated between young and old. It was the tyranny of youth in action. If you had varicose veins, cellulite, or any other of the dermal afflictions of age, you couldn't be on the thigh-baring cutting edge. As Quant's husband and business partner, Alexander Plunket Greene, so bluntly declared: "Many [Quant fashions] shouldn't be worn by people over twenty-eight."

And there you had it. Gnash your dentures at the injustice of it all—or better, scowl censoriously at the kicky, miniskirted "birds" skipping along the King's Road in London—but the fact would remain that, if you were over thirty, you probably weren't happening. Never mind that Mr. Greene himself was then thirty-three (and a cheeky male to boot, who couldn't suffer the iniquity of the miniskirt firsthand); as one of the vanguard he was age-proof, or for that matter all the more exalted—"an elder statesman of the Mod movement," as the New York Times described him.

What was Mod? Well, Mod was short for "modern," of course, but it meant a lot more than that. It went beyond the harsh fact of the miniskirt or the porkpie hats and foppish, "continental" fashions sported by Mod men. It was, like so many of the lifestyles to which youth of the Sixties conformed (in the fanciful act of not conforming), a fully co-opted "movement," with its own evolving code of behavior and dress. And though by mid-decade most of the western world aspired to Mod-ernity, it was specifically a movement of the British working class.

As Pete Townshend of the rock group The Who described it: "The Mod movement in England…was a movement of young people, much bigger than the hippies and the underground…To be a Mod you had to have short hair, money enough to buy a real smart suit, good shoes, good shirts, plenty of pills all the time, and a scooter covered with lamps—and you had to be able to dance like a madman….As a force, they were unbelievable. They were the Bulge, the result of all the old soldiers coming back from war and screwing until they were blue in the face. Thousands and thousands of kids—too many kids, not enough teachers, not enough parents, not enough pills to go around. The feeling of being a Mod among two million mods was incredible."

It was in class-conscious England then, that baby-boomers of the Sixties made their most definable impact, disrupting the status quo not only as a movement of uppity, omnipresent youth, but as uppity proles who at last had the spending power and sheer force of numbers needed to gain the socio-economic upper hand. In an April 1966 cover story, Time hailed London as "the city of the decade," gushing over the ascendance of a "swinging meritocracy" composed of artists, singers, photographers, and miscellaneous East End yobs who were forcing the old aristocracy out. London, according to Time, was "a sparkling, slapdash comedy…a dazzling blur…buzzing…pulsing …spinning." The American cover girl/starlet Baby Jane Holzer (dubbed "The Girl of the Year" in 1964 by Tom Wolfe) captured the excitement of Swinging London in her own giddy terms: "When Mick [Jagger] comes into the Ad Lib in London—I mean, there's nothing like the Ad Lib in New York. You can go to the Ad Lib and everybody is there. They're all young, and they're taking over, it's like a whole revolution. I mean, it's exciting, they're all from the lower classes, East End-sort-of-thing. There's nobody exciting from the upper classes anymore…."

The hegemony of Anglicized youth, along with some of its more interesting consequences, may be illustrated by a distant episode from mid-Sixties Rio: when a miniskirted girl crossed her legs on a bus, the sixty-three-year-old man beside her sagged over and bit her on the thigh. This sad protest on behalf of left-out sexagenarians the world over was punished with a three-day jail sentence.

From the late Fifties to the early Sixties, British working-class teenagers were largely divided into two basic groups, the Mods and the Rockers. The latter was the more delinquent of the two (no small claim), sporting leather jackets and greasy hair and rumbling about London on enormous "ton-up" motorcycles—a far cry from the Vespa minibikes favored by Mods, which prompted sneering Rockers to label them "scooter boys." In both cases, having their own forms of transportation was key to the glorious image of Rebellious Youth—not only did it enhance a sense of independence, but it looked good to the birds, too (who, it was hoped, were wont to notice one's resemblance to Marlon Brando in The Wild One).

No tribal rivalry being complete without the occasional rumble, Mods and Rockers made it a point to beat each other up whenever possible. This had to be more distasteful to the Mods, whose sine qua non was a meticulous, stream-lined wardrobe: high-collared jackets and thin black ties, stove-pipe pants, and high-peaked hats. Perhaps to com-pensate, Mods also wore hard, pointy-toed boots, the better to deliver a lethal swipe to some Rocker's crotch.

By the mid-Sixties, Rockers were reduced to a sullen fringe group, while the amoral, pill-popping Mods were transformed into mainstream madcaps, and finally a worldwide phenomenon, thanks mostly to the machinations of a single man, the Svengali of the Beatles, Brian Epstein. Before Epstein, the Beatles had been a thuggish bunch of yobs from Liverpool, affecting the leather, sideburns, and Crisco hair typical of their class and origin. In this incarnation, John, Paul, George, Pete Best, and Stu Sutcliffe played some of the roughest rock-and-roll clubs in Hamburg, Germany, dodging beer bottles and exchanging drunken obscenities with their rowdy greaser fans. Epstein, who signed the Beatles to a management contract in 1962, effected a miraculous rehabilitation, changing their image down to the merest detail—even the proletarian Woodbine cigarettes had to go, exchanged for the suaver Senior Service brand. Pete Best and Stu Sutcliffe left the group, replaced by the teddy-bearish Ringo Starr.

The new Beatles embodied all that was fun loving and fab, with their long (but shampooed) hair and Mod gray lounge-suits with skinny black lapels. If they rebelled, they did so only with wacky, hyperactive high jinks and the ever-ready bit of cheek for the media, their quips sprinkled with such endearing Liverpool colloquialisms as "hey, luv" and "very fooney, mate." The onstage performances were full of yeah-yeah-yeah perkiness, their faces beaming with cherubic, well-scrubbed cheer, their fluffy Beatle bangs tossed about with zany "I'm-yoong!-I'm-reech!" abandon. They became luvable ideals to all the giddy birds coming of age in reborn, ultra-mod London, as well as beacons of hope to every loutish lad pining away for the big time. The Beatles were living proof that the young had inherited the earth, and that London was the loverly hub of the whole swinging universe.

Under the headline, BEATLEMANIA! YEAH! YEAH! YEAH!, an editorial in the London Daily Mirror reported: "Beatle people [are] everywhere. From Wapping to Windsor. Aged seven to seventy. And it's plain to see why these four cheeky, energetic lads from Liverpool go down so big. They're young, new. They're high-spirited, cheerful." At a November 1963 Royal-Command Performance, the queen mother was seen stomping her feet; Princess Margaret became so carried away by "Twist and Shout" that she started clapping her hands to the beat. Most smitten of all, understandably enough, was the teenage Prince Charles: when the press took note of his unroyally shaggy hairdo, the young prince rejoined that he'd been wearing a Beatles cut since he was two years old. Fab!

By 1966, worldwide Anglophilia had risen to a laughably swinging fever-pitch, even though the crabby old guard did its best to rise against the occasion, to stem the degenerate tide of long hair and high hemlines. Stringent new codes of dress and grooming were institutionally enforced: in North America and Britain, schoolgirls were made to pass a "kneeling test"— if a girl's hem failed to touch the floor when she kneeled, she was expelled on the spot; in Vatican City and sunny old Athens, wearing a miniskirt was actually against the law. When out on the town with their mates, young male office workers had to resort to mop-top wigs or Dutchboy caps to conceal the humiliatingly close-cropped haircuts their stern employers forced upon them. It was a thoroughly grotty situation, to be sure, but with a little help from their friends in commerce, youth would go on being served.

As ever, the United States outdid the world in exploiting the latest youth craze. For Americans, mod London fashions were as close as one's mailbox, via the Montgomery Ward "Carnaby Street Boutique" catalog or the "Brolly Male" collection by McGregor, which offered such startlingly "gear" items as Liverpool Flame bell-bottoms ("Edwardian updated to fit the brawny American"), with a rise guaranteed to be no more than four inches (10 cm) from inseam to belt. And as mod fashions gravitated more and more toward bizarre neo-"Edwardian" parody—frilly cuffs, fat polka-dotted ties, flare-bottomed trousers—eager Yanks became more dizzily British than the British themselves. Thousands of teenagers lined up outside Stern Brothers department store in Chicago for a show of John Stephens' Carnaby Street fashions, while local retailers puzzled and delighted over the fact that Windy City teens were willing to spend their entire allowances in a strenuous effort to look British.

Ever since February 1964, when an army of shrieking moppets stormed Kennedy Airport to welcome the Beatles, British music had ruled the North American airwaves, and a number of deejays had mysteriously acquired British accents—throwing in a lot of "jolly goods" and "old chaps" for the sake of authenticity. The first wave of such "Mersey Beat" bands as Gerry and the Pacemakers, Peter and Gordon, the Dave Clark Five, and Herman's Hermits, followed closely in the Beatles' tracks, adopting the image of cuddly, luv-struck ragamuffins, with treacly hits like "Mrs. Brown You've Got a Lovely Daughter," "A World Without Love," and "Glad All Over." The backlash came in the form of rebellious anti-Beatles groups such as the Rolling Stones, the Animals, the Kinks, and the Who, the last of which took pains to trash a new set of instruments at each and every performance.

Everybody wanted a piece of the action. Mod wanna-be's from all over the world bought youth-fare tickets and took off

for London—a nightmarish pseudo-Edwardian mob of them surging into Carnaby Street and the King's Road, thousands of squawking transistor radios heralding their arrival. Boutiques such as Mary Quant's Bazaar became hangouts for the touristy young—"like a youth club," said The New York Times, "where the customer could find friendly advice, a congenial atmosphere, as well as realistic clothes at cheap prices." Well, cheap anyway; but the clothes became more fantastic daily, as designers tried frantically to top themselves, to be more zany, more youthful, to be gloriously, transcendently Mod! The London Daily Express sounded a vaguely worried note at the beginning of 1967: "Any fine Saturday you can see the full…fancy dress parade. The effect is strange, not really horrific if properly done, but the mind boggles at what could happen."

And happen it did. Unappeased by the planefuls of cash pouring into old Chelsea, Quant and her husband Alexander Plunket Greene toured the States, received by throngs of rabid consumers wherever they went. No slouch at self-promotion, Greene would virtually take over local radio stations, playing 'round-the-clock Beatles music and rhapsodizing between records (his Cockney accent pushed to its gruesome limit) about the gear life of Swinging London.

Heeding the call, tourists invaded London in a final, feral blitz, driven by visions of the hip hoi polloi at the Ad-Lib, A-Train, or Ska Bar, yearning to catch a glimpse of "Mick" (Jagger again) sipping his morning espresso at the Guys and Dolls Coffee House in Chelsea, as was his custom (or so Time assured its readers—never mind that Mick rarely, if ever, got out of bed before noon and was, by then, better "glimpsed" at Max's Kansas City or The Scene in New York). What they did glimpse, if not the trendy "meritocracy"—who were a step ahead of them, i.e. elsewhere, like Mick—was a city whose very physical shape had changed with the mod upheaval: Chelsea's charming eighteenth-century atmosphere had all but vanished, mod-ernized into a cheesy farrago of boutiques, record, souvenir, and secondhand shops, all of it loud with music and nattering tourists. Much of the slate-and-chimney skyline was gone too, made over

THE ROLLING STONES POSE FOR AN EARLY PUBLICITY PHOTO.

© LDE/Archive Photos

into such bustling cityscapes as Centre Point, proudly called the "first pop-art office block" of London. The later Prince Charles, quite drained of all moddishness, would spend much of his time off the polo field railing against the foul urban architecture which sprang up during the Sixties, and which no one since has had the good manners to raze.

Just as the Beatles had helped to usher in the mod era, so they ushered it out. With their Sgt. Pepper's Lonely Hearts Club Band album in 1967 they committed themselves to psychedelia, becoming disciples of the

Maharishi Mahesh Yogi and abandoning forever the mop-top image. Professor Timothy Leary, blown away by the "profundity" of the Sgt. Pepper album, declared the Beatles "the wisest, holiest, most effective avatars the human race has ever produced."

No longer was London the "city of the decade." Eric Burdon of the Animals said it all when he urged his English brothers and sisters to "save up all your bread and fly Trans-Love Airways to San Francisco.…There's no place left to go." In a world plagued by war and moddish materialism, the gentle hippies seemed the last best hope.

THE BEATLES CHUCK THEIR CHEEKY, MAD-CAP ANTICS FOR THE MELLOWER WAYS OF THE MAHARISHI— AND THE WORLD FOLLOWS SUIT.

The Drug Culture

Ah, to be young (seventeen to twenty-five years old, demographically speaking), middle class, disaffected, and white in the summer of '67, the Summer of Love, when all the flower people were going to come together once and for all and establish a new order based on peace, love, and eastern mysticism. There you'd be an enlightened dropout—having had *some* college education (along with 68 percent of your brothers and sisters) before chucking the whole bourgeois scene—slumped on a stoop in the "Hashbury"...picturing yourself, perhaps, in a boat on a river, with tangerine trees and marmalade skies...when suddenly, through a purplish haze of exhaust, upsetting utterly the Oneness of it all, appears a jouncing Gray Line Bus coming to take you away on the popular "Hippie Hop" sightseeing tour through San Francisco's Haight-Ashbury district.

"You are passing through the Bearded Curtain," the tour guide intones, as the bus crawls alongside your stoop. "Marijuana is a household staple here, enjoyed by the natives to stimulate the senses."

A middle-aged Ohioan couple taps at the bus window and begins to wave...at you! Yes, you—a true native, a lovably freakish fellow. One of them makes a "peace sign" for your benefit. Mortified by this invasion of squares, you take a sullen drag off your reefer—but the spiel goes on:

"Among the favorite pastimes of the hippies, besides taking drugs, are parading and demonstrating; seminars and group discussions about what's wrong with the status quo; malingering; plus the ever-present preoccupation with the soul, reality, and self-expression, such as strumming guitars, piping flutes, and banging on bongos...."

Blearily, you're thinking: "We don't parade—we drop out! ...And what's this about 'bongos'? We're not beatniks, man, that was the Fif—"

And then you're granted a minor epiphany—and you see yourself as the Ohioans see you: a picturesque middle-class white kid (whether beatnik or hipnik or flipnik) going through a "phase," draped in the same adorable kaftan that the Campbell's Soup tykes are sporting in all the magazine ads. You try to get back to the subject of Oneness, but what really occurs to you is the Oneness of mass media: of "psychedelic" Peter Max posters, socks, wallpaper, clocks; of the souvenir headshops, boutiques, and health-food eateries that have sprouted up and down Haight Street; and of Sammy Davis, Jr., wearing a Nehru jacket and beads on "The Mike Douglas Show." You sigh as the whole gleeful busload waves farewell as One....Oh, wow.

"Tune in, turn on, drop out," said LSD-guru Timothy Leary, once of Harvard. For a number of baby-boomers, bored to death with complacent affluence, repelled by a corrupt, war-mongering government, and enticed Id-ward by such role models as the moose-lipped Mick Jagger (sweaty, shirtless, getting no satisfaction), Professor Leary's message had clear appeal. It came down to a choice, or so it seemed at the time, between attaining Cosmic Consciousness while partaking of free love and loud music or going the way of the Establishment—meaning one job, one mate, and eventual retirement in safe, piggy Suburbia, parked in front on a television set. Easy choice, really, when put like that, and not without a certain quixotic grandeur. No wonder so many baby-boomers today tend to wax nostalgic—dusting off those old Procol Harum records, smoking that occasional joint with the spouse, another day nearer oblivion.

"Hey, at least we cared in those days, man!" some compromised true believers may still say (prior to a long, muddled silence).

To paraphrase the Elvis Costello song, What exactly was so funny about peace, love, and understanding? Was it, perhaps, the irony of having to be stoned all the time?

Though pot smoking had been *de rigueur* among hip white counterculturalists throughout the Fifties (appropriated, along with the entire Hip concept, from black jazz musicians), the recreational-cum-visionary properties of LSD were not widely appreciated until the Sixties. Professor Leary began his crusade by giving students "psychedelic lessons" in 1960, amid the earnestly Eastern ambience of his Psychodrama Room: Hindu ragas on the hi-fi, candlelit Buddha posters, and the beatific Leary himself, sprawled upon a mattress. When Harvard gave him the boot in 1962 (objecting more to the messianic flakiness of it all than to LSD *per se,* which was then still legal), Leary founded the League for Spiritual Discovery and set out around the country to spread the good word—to wit, "You Have to Be Out of Your Mind to Pray."

Author Ken Kesey, meanwhile, discovered LSD as a paid volunteer in a government experiment with "psychomimetic" drugs at the Menlo Park Veteran's Hospital. Impressed, Kesey continued experimenting on his own time, taking a job as night attendant in the hospital's psychiatric ward and often presiding over his charges in a hallucinatory funk. From these experiences he wrote his most famous novel, One Flew Over the Cuckoo's Nest (1962), into which he incorporated stream-of-consciousness passages written under the influence of peyote.

A charismatic figure, Kesey parlayed his literary success into notoriety as the zany leader of the Merry Pranksters, a group of LSD devotees. In 1964, on completing his second novel, Sometimes a Great Notion, Kesey bought a 1939 International Harvester school bus which he and his followers painted in lurid psychedelic swirls. The destination sign read FURTHER, while a sign in back read CAUTION: WEIRD LOAD. Finally, equipped with movie cameras and sophisticated sound equipment, the Pranksters embarked on a cross-country, "acid"-fueled trip to New York. Their mission, as Kesey stated it, went something like this: "Everybody is going to be what they are, and whatever they are, there's not going to be anything to apologize about. What we are, we're going to wail with on this whole trip."

So the Pranksters wore superhero regalia (Day-Glo capes, goggles, American flags) and assumed such nicknames as Swashbuckler (Kesey), Zonker, Mountain Girl, Mal Function, and Speed (a.k.a. Neal Cassady, the "Dean Moriarty" character in Jack Kerouac's On the Road), and bent themselves to the task of freaking out the Squares. One of their more inspired pranks occurred in Phoenix,

© Wide World Photos

Arizona, the hometown of arch-conservative presidential candidate Barry Goldwater, where they put a banner on the bus reading, A VOTE FOR BARRY IS A VOTE FOR FUN! and sped backward down the city's main drag.

This pilgrimage, however, like the hippie movement it helped to inspire, turned gradually into a bummer. The sheer bodily discomfort of it all (the long ride in a ramshackle bus, the ghastly summer heat, the proximity of so many unbathed proto-hippies, and of course the nonstop drug-taking) got to be a problem. As Tom Wolfe described it in The Electric Kool-Aid Acid Test (his "nonfiction novel" about Kesey and the Merry Pranksters): "Nobody can sleep so they keep taking more speed to keep going…and then smoke grass to take the goddamn tachycardiac edge off the speed, and acid to make the whole thing turn into something else." Nor, in such a state of general malaise, did human relations tend to flourish—and in this particular respect the joyride proved prophetic, a microcosmic foreglimpse of the Haight-Ashbury in the late Sixties. As Barry Leeds wrote in his study of Kesey: "The portrait which emerges [from Wolfe's book] is

KEN "SWASHBUCKLER" KESEY, WHOSE MERRY PRANKSTERS PROVIDED A PILL-POPPING PARADIGM FOR THE WHOLE HIPPIE MOVEMENT. ABOVE, KESEY PREPARES TO DELIVER HIS BUS TO THE SMITHSONIAN IN 1990, THUS BELATEDLY DOING HIS PART FOR THE ESTABLISHMENT.

a horrific one, in which rivalries, defections, paranoia, and nervous breakdowns are rampant. The atmosphere inside the bus seems more often hysterical than merry, infernal rather than ecstatic."

For Kesey, the Wisdom of the Bus amounted to this: acid is better enjoyed in a controlled environment. So began a series of "acid tests" staged by the Pranksters at parties throughout San Francisco's Bay Area, at which great vats of LSD-spiked (hence "electric") Kool-Aid were served to bring about mind-expansion on a truly righteous scale. As LSD was still something of a novelty, many partygoers drank the Kool-Aid without knowing that it served any purpose other than quenching thirst—which was part of the plan. That is, veteran acidheads such as Kesey were then able to observe, ethnologist-like, the spectacle of hundreds, thousands of "first time flyers" staring ingenuously, say, at their hands (a flower!) or at the friendly lizard nipping at their toes.

The true mastermind behind most of these capers was one Augustus Owsley Stanley III, the "LSD Chemist" who supplied Kesey's acid-tests by way of establishing his own considerable fame. Owsley, the son of a United States senator from Kentucky, had the entrepreneurial foresight to buy 500 grams of lysergic acid monohydrate (the basic ingredient of LSD) from the Cycle Chemical Corporation for $20,000, which he then converted into 1.5 million doses at $2 a pop, retail. Newsweek called him "the Henry Ford of LSD," and Owsley's product was regarded both in North America and abroad as nonpareil, the absolute Dom Perignon of acid. "This is real Owsley acid," connoisseurs would nudge each other.

But Owsley was more than just a wily businessman; like Kesey and Leary, he fancied himself a great liberator of sorts, whose mission it was to help the benighted masses grope their way toward enlightenment. It was rumored that Owsley manufactured his incomparable dope with the help of the occult, no less, muttering obscure incantations over the chemicals. Teenie Weenie Deanie (sic), one of Owsley's lab assistants, remembers his awe upon visiting "The Maestro's" suburban headquarters for the first time:

"Descending the basement stairs was like entering a psychedelic spaceship. The walls were covered with machinery and bubbling flasks, coiled glass tubes dripping potential weirdness from container to container, floor to ceiling. Huge glass cauldrons surrounded with dry ice covered the floor, oozing white clouds of spacey vapors into the room. 'Very serious business' flashed through my brain."

Perhaps the most enduring of Owsley's accomplishments was his part in creating the "acid rock" sound of The Grateful Dead, whose jam sessions formed the mind-blowing aural backdrop to those seminal acid-tests. Owsley, an electronics freak, devised a sound system of such hyper-amplification as to render all human speech (itself an elusive concept to tripping acidheads) impossible. This was an epochal development in the history of rock and roll.

But it was Owsley's prowess in eluding the law that contributed most to his legend. When LSD and other hallucinogens were declared illegal in 1966, Owsley became the drug underworld's most celebrated outlaw. (Kesey, it should be noted, had fled to Mexico to avoid arrest, later re-entering the United States disguised as a drunken cowboy-singer, riding past bemused border guards on a horse; he was arrested by the FBI a month later.) A favorite Owsley campfire story told how the Maestro was once pulled over en route to San Francisco with a jar of his purest LSD. When the policeman inquired about the jar's contents, Owsley invited him to taste it and find out. The cop took a swig; then, satisfied that it was nothing but water (LSD is tasteless), he sent Owsley on his way. Owsley drove around a curve and waited. Moments later the saucer-eyed fuzz went flying off the road into the Pacific Ocean, galvanized by about 10,000 hits of *haute* Owsley Acid.

In 1968, Owsley was caught in possession of 868,000 doses. Though his lawyers argued that the LSD was strictly for his own use, Owsley was sentenced to a full three years in jail.

By 1965 a sensibility of sorts was forming among Bay Area acidheads. They began to conceive their lifestyle in terms of a full-blown Mellow Utopia, and San Francisco's Haight-Ashbury district fell nearest the mark. Unlike the folkniks and activists of the Berkeley Left, denizens of the emerging Haight subculture were not concerned much with changing the System, which, they figured, would fall of its own rottenness. Rather, they yearned for a kind of *anti*-system based on, well, letting it happen…whether "it" be sex, drugs, rock and roll, or the serenity that arose from indulging in all three—an essentially nonpolitical, non-intellectual approach, at any rate.

Berkeley radicals, for their part, took a dim view of the Haight. When poet Allen Ginsberg introduced the term "Flower Power" at a 1965 Berkeley antiwar rally, a wary grumble passed through the crowd. In the wake of the campus Free Speech Movement, and all the heady publicity that went with it, Berkeley had grown protective of its stature as the red-hot center of youthful unrest. And yet somehow, insidiously, the spotlight was shifting. The San Francisco Examiner on September 6, 1965 heralded A NEW PARADISE FOR BEATNIKS, specifically referring to the Blue Unicorn coffeehouse, a "new hip hangout" in the Haight. It was in this article that reporter Michael Fallon coined the term "hippies," which conferred a sort of wacky benignity upon the acidheads who congregated there. In another account the hippies were described as "bearded philosophers."

Philosophers, forsooth! Such pretensions were an outrage to Berkeley politicos. For one thing, the hippies were not engaged (or *engagé,* as the Sartre-versed radical liked to say), politically or otherwise; they had no agenda, other than whatever was implied by "Oh, wow." Worst of all was the hippies' wholehearted endorsement of rock and roll, which to the Left embodied all that was frivolous and "commercial" about the nation's youth; folk, with its somber ballads about Building a Better World, was the only unimpeachably "correct" music.

Berkeley's sense of countercultural preeminence was pretty much blown out of the water in 1966, beginning with the Trips Festival at San Francisco's Longshoremen's Hall. "The Haight-Ashbury era was born that weekend," Tom Wolfe declared. The Trips Festival was the most colossal acid-test yet: LSD was everywhere—in the punch, the cake, the ice cream, and in tab-filled bags floating freely about the hall. Moreover, a definitive tripping milieu was established: ultraviolet lights turning the skin a groovy glowing green, strobe-lights freezing frames of motion so that, snapping your eyes shut, you could watch the moment slowly dissolve, megasonic waves of righteous rock and roll, provided by such avatars as The Grateful Dead and Big Brother & the Holding Company. Most incredible were the consummate vibes of the place, everyone tripping at once, thousands and thousands of 'heads, all one big happy mind-expanded family. No more the existential bummer of being one of a few lone miscreants, huddled in some squalid (albeit gloriously unbourgeois) crash-pad. The festival offered the possibility of a "cause," perhaps even a movement: yes, no doubt about it—look around, wall-to-wall acidheads!—the hippies were happening, all right.

All over the country, more and more young people decided they were disenchanted, anti-establishment, and so on, and thus migrated to the Haight. They spilled onto the streets, crashing on sidewalks and in doorways. Musicians and whatnot abounded: non-hippie pedestrians were asked to cough up a little bread in exchange for impromptu guitar, flute, or tambourine recitals. Poetic readings of some of the heavier Beatles lyrics were given. Everyone panhandled and, in principle, everyone shared—joints, tabs of acid, spare change, bits of food. It was beautiful.

A lot of hippies had dogs, which naturally were allowed to run loose. These bandanna-clad hiphounds enhanced the Haight's Garden of Eden mystique: "humans and animals like, together, man—innocent and free!" Of course, there were droppings all over the place, and the stench was, for a fact, mind blowing. But, hey—that too was beautiful. As Burton Wolfe wrote in his book, The Hippies: "Several times, I saw barefoot hippie girls squish their toes into a big pile of dog excrement, calmly walk to the curb, and scrape it off like you would from your shoe. 'I used to worry about things like that before I took LSD,' one of them told me. 'Now my mind

Anything seemed possible: there was much talk—weirdly credible talk—about the new "alternative society" that was forming amid the ashes of the poor old United States. The Millenium (a nonchronological catchword for the New Age, the Age of Aquarius, or what you will) appeared to be at hand. But first, youth had to put its own house in order, and this meant healing the rift between apolitical Hashburians and the cranky radicals of the Berkeley left. Nothing less than mass catharsis would do; hence the San Francisco Human Be-In of 1967.

"Berkeley activists and the love generation of the Haight-Ashbury will join together with members of the new nation who will be coming from every state in the nation, every tribe of the young (the emerging soul of the nation) to powwow, celebrate, and prophesy the epoch of liberation, love, peace, compassion, and unity of mankind."

So went the press conference on January 12, 1967; two days later it happened.

Charles Perry, a writer for Rolling Stone, remembers being able to feel "cosmic reverberations from all the LSD being dropped":

> The closer we got to the Polo Field, the more we saw; tributaries of walkers flowing into larger and larger streams. There were lots of smiles, the unique Be-In smile, at once conspiratorial, caressing, astonished and beaming with stoned-out optimism. We'd left automobiles out in the streets, along with middle-aged hostiles, General Westmoreland and the whole dead-end culture....A lot of stoned people were wandering around blowing their minds on how many others were there. It was like awakening to find you'd been reborn and this was your new family.

has opened, and I see that it's all part of life: dirt, feces, everything. Feces are groovy!'"

For the hippies there really was a kind of "brief shining moment," lasting roughly from 1966 to the summer of 1967, when they might have had a beneficent effect on the world. The whole thing was, in an obscure way, working; whatever its hygienic failures, the Haight tended to be a peaceful, kindly community. Rather than hold loud demonstrations and otherwise provoke the "pigs," they celebrated togetherness—they got placidly stoned at street fairs, rock concerts, festivals. There were, of course, flowers in their hair. They meditated. California bishop James Pike observed: "There is something about the temper of these people, a gentleness, a quietness, an interest—something good."

As from some feel-good zombie movie, an estimated 20,000 Humans converged on Golden Gate Park, arriving from all over the nation to…what? "Powwow"? "Prophesy"? Well, sure, though most were too zonked to get past the smiling part. Things happened in fits and starts. Allen

Ginsberg chanted the mantra of Shiva ("the god of dynamite hashish," Perry points out) and people did their best to chant along. Leary mounted the stage and started with his "Tune in, turn on, drop out" spiel—which may have struck that crowd as a bit redundant. The Grateful Dead got people dancing, though in broad daylight (lacking strobes) the dancers looked like so many fish, floppily expiring.

But mostly people roamed. Roamed and smiled. The food was free, the acid was free (delivered by Owsley, who parachuted in and disappeared), and the entertainment was free. There were only two policemen on hand, knitting their brows at proffered flowers. When it was over, the hippies cleared all the debris and left the Polo Field just as they'd found it—almost as if they'd never been there at all.

"The press would go bananas in the next days trying to figure out what this event was about," wrote Perry. "It would become one of the grand mythic elements of the Haight… along with indiscriminate love and the anonymity of the Diggers [Hippie social-workers]—the notion of meeting without any purpose other than to be. Together."

Suffice it to say that the Be-In was probably the high point of the hippie era.

"A great butterfly had emerged and taken wing in the setting sun of the San Francisco Human Be-In," wrote Gene Anthony in The Summer of Love. "It flew across the land, then on across the sea to other continents. Wherever that psychedelic butterfly touched down to earth, its spirit captured the consciousness of masses of young people."

By the look of things in 1967, that butterfly was spending a lot of time on Madison Avenue, Carnaby Street, and points east. Certainly the "consciousness" of the world media was captured: one could hardly buy a loaf of whole wheat bread without there being some psychedelic angle—a cartoon hippie on the wrapper, say, whose word bubble touted the loaf's macrobiotic purity. There were hippie dolls (a ball of fur, shades, and a crazed grin), body-painting kits, back-to-nature cookbooks, "Eastern" paraphernalia of every sort (hookah pipes, incense burners, plastic sitars, silly clothes), and an avalanche of decals, posters, and toys. When Mr.

Anthony wrote of the "masses of young people," did he mean children ages three through twelve? Evidently so, for the butterfly was there too, flapping atop towheaded tots everywhere. Even G. I. Joe went groovy, what with his afro, beard, and look of strange composure about the eyes and mouth.

The fashion world was all agog. The nutty, dustbin motley of the great unwashed was refined into a "look" sought by debutantes and dropouts alike. Bell-bottom jeans, sold pre-faded and pre-tattered, were key to the overall effect—proof that the wearer had a "with-it" sense of solidarity, whether or not one opted for the whole grungy flower-child scene. The rest of the ensemble told the difference, however: whereas "real" hippies tended to live in the clothes they stood up in, however dank and reeking, the merely "with-in" went in for all sorts of sequins and convoluted embroidery, silks, and plush velvet—dearly bought on The Portobello Road or Carnaby Street in London, or perhaps in the Haight itself, in the new boutiques that real hippies were loath to enter.

As the Summer of Love drew nigh, the flight of youths to the Haight took on a decidedly sinister aspect. With their feckless groping for some sort of panacea, each new wave of pilgrims seemed a little more fishy than the one before. Original settlers were already wistful for the good old days, when they were still a cozy subculture and not yet a mega-hyped national phenomenon. And things were about to get worse: Newsweek predicted a "flash flood" of aspirant hippies in June, when schools let out.

Sure enough, they came in droves, drawn mostly by rumors of wild, druggy sex, devoid of the lofty "spiritual values" which hitherto had been the Haight's redemption. And this in turn was a cue for the pushers, pimps, prostitutes, perverts, and needle-freaks to move in, turning the place into a veritable caravansary of street scum. While the Gray Line Bus brought its daily cargo of gawking innocents through the "Bearded Curtain," Diggers were busy distributing leaflets: BY AUGUST HAIGHT STREET WILL BE A CEMETARY. The Summer of Love had dawned, all right, presided over by a psychedelic pterodactyl come home to roost.

PROMOTIONAL POSTER FOR THE FAMOUS FILLMORE AUDITORIUM—SO "PSYCHEDELIC" IN DESIGN THAT YOU ALMOST HAVE TO BE AN ACID-HEAD TO READ IT.

Paul Caruso Collection

HIPPIE TYKES AT THE
HOG FARM COMMUNE
IN NEW MEXICO
ADAPT GAMELY TO
THE SQUALOR OF
RURAL LIFE.

© Lisa Law

Less than ten months after the Millennial promise of the Human Be-In, a more solemn procession made its way through Golden Gate Park, this time in order to bring the Haight-Ashbury era to its ceremonial conclusion. After a summer of "murder, rape, racial clashes, and uncontrolled drug taking" (so Newsweek reported), Ron Thelin of the Haight's Psychedelic Shop announced "The Death of Hippie —Beloved Son of Mass Media." An hirsute effigy laden with beads, peacock feathers, marijuana cookies, and other hippie accoutrements was brought to the park in a casket and burned.

Many flower children were already casualties of The Summer of Love, comatose, psychotic, or bound to the Haight by speed and/or heroin addiction that would claim them sooner or later. The "Death of Hippie" mourners lingered around the pyre, contemplating their next move. Ever given to prophetic statement, hippies were now predicting that a great earthquake was imminent—that all of California would be plunged into the sea. A hippie diaspora was hence imperative: some would move to the country, others would join religious cults, antiwar factions, or, alas, the dreaded Establishment, cutting their hair and heading home. "Thus, last week, in the mecca of mindlessness did the hippies proclaim their own demise," Time announced gleefully.

But such reports were at least somewhat exaggerated. Many hippie diehards rounded out the Sixties at such communes as The Hog Farm, New Buffalo, Arroyo Seco, and Canyoncito, places where kindred spirits built huts, pitched tents, and lived off the land. They baked bread that was oh-so-dark and spawned families in their own image: great packs of sprawling, tousle-haired, barefoot urchins dancing through the dog droppings as in days of old. As Jane and Michael Stern describe the scene in Sixties People:

> Country paradise, hippie style, was like a vision of Indian life from some old Hollywood movie in which...tribesmen in buckskin fringe sit around their teepees smoking pipes, beating tom-toms, and speaking in portentous homilies, while the squaws (bare-breasted, natch) tend the babies and make dinner in elegantly primitive huts.

For a while it seemed like the ideally righteous rebuff to rat-race society. One could have one's macrobiotic cake and eat it too. Minus the bourgeois head trip, hippies enjoyed such conventional perks as marriage, children, and even religion. (Christianity, in fact, was making a big comeback among hippies. The Reverend Arthur Blessit, a tireless proselytizer of hippies, urged them to "turn on to a trip with an everlasting high—Jesus, man. He won't hassle you.") After all, many flower children were getting on in years, relatively speaking, and even at its best the Haight had been no place to raise a family. But in the country they could be self-sufficient and Together as never before, all of them grooving on the bread and beans, the homegrown grass, and caring for each other's broods.

One may remember that scene in Easy Rider when Wyatt and Billy stop at the commune: a bad summer has parched the crops and left the hippies (all the more saintly in hardship) on their collective last leg. And so it went. In the end, most hippies just weren't cut out for the morbidities of bucolia—in light of which, air-conditioned suburbia began to look not so bad, nor even so boring: at least a nine-to-five job gave you something to do.

The Establishment had the last laugh in a big way. Long after "Hippie" had been cremated in Golden Gate Park, and the Haight had gone the way of Atlantis, the merry manipulators of mass media continued to get a chuckle at the hippies' expense. Mondo Hippie merchandise continued to move of its own kitschy momentum, especially the clothes, transmogrifying into the polyester-and-sideburns look of the Seventies. "Laugh-In," the big television hit of 1968, milked the moribund movement for all it was worth: Arte Johnson appeared as a daffy, Nehru-jacketed soothsayer, and Goldie Hawn as a frugging flower girl, her body painted top to bottom with inane psychedelia.

Perhaps the final conk to the hippies' bushy noggins was the musical Hair, which put an unprecedented sixteen of twenty-six songs on the singles charts and went on to become one of the top-five moneymakers in Broadway history. Billed as "an American tribal love-rock musical," Hair succeeded more as a diabolical capitalist parody than as a "celebration" of hippie mores. Its fame rested mostly on a single scene, in which bewigged, Dionysiac cast-members flung off their clothes and entreated the audience to "Swing with us! Turn on with us!"

On hearing of the show's then-exorbitant ticket price, the seventy-three-year-old Groucho Marx got undressed in front of a mirror and stared at himself for a few minutes.

"This isn't worth eleven bucks," he concluded.

© Central Press/Archive Photos

"SWING WITH US! TURN ON WITH US!" THE PSEUDO-HIPPIE CAST OF HAIR IMPLORES ITS BEMUSED AUDIENCE.

BIBLIOGRAPHY

Armstrong, Neil. First on the Moon. Little, Brown 1970.

Baez, Joan. And a Voice to Sing With. Summit 1987.

Bloom, Allan. The Closing of the American Mind. Simon & Schuster 1987.

Bradlee, Benjamin. Conversations with Kennedy. Norton 1975.

Cleaver, Eldridge. Soul on Ice. Dell 1968.

Clifford, Clark. Counsel to the President. Random House 1991.

Cluster, Dick, ed. They Should Have Served that Cup of Coffee: Seven Radicals Remember the Sixties. South End Press 1979.

Collier, Peter, and David Horowitz. The Kennedys: An American Drama. Summit 1984.

Davies, Hunter. The Beatles. McGraw-Hill 1985.

Desaulniers, Louise, ed. 119 Years of the Atlantic. Little, Brown 1977.

Golson, Barry, ed. The Playboy Interview. Wideview Books 1981.

Gottlieb, Annie. Do You Believe in Magic? The Second Coming of the Sixties Generation. Random House 1987.

Grun, Bernard. The Timetables of History. Simon & Schuster 1975.

Halberstam, David. The Best and the Brightest. Random House 1972.

Harris, Nathaniel. The Sixties: An Illustrated History. Macdonald Educational 1975.

Hendler, Herb. Year by Year in the Rock Era. Greenwood Press 1983.

Kennedy, Robert F. Thirteen Days: Cuban Missile Crisis. Norton 1969.

Kovic, Ron. Born on the Fourth of July. McGraw-Hill 1976.

King, Martin Luther, Jr. Where Do We Go from Here: Chaos or Community? Harper & Row 1967.

Kunen, James. The Strawberry Statement: Notes of a College Revolutionary. Random House 1969.

Levin, Bernard. The Pendulum Years: Britain in the Sixties. Cape 1970.

Miller, Jim, ed. The Rolling Stone Illustrated History of Rock and Roll. Random House/ Rolling Stone Press 1976.

Nabokov, Vladimir. Strong Opinions. McGraw-Hill 1973.

Obst, Lynda, ed. The Sixties. Random House/ Rolling Stone Press 1977.

Peck, Abe. Uncovering the Sixties: The Life and Times of the Radical Press. Pantheon 1985.

Perry, Charles. The Haight-Ashbury: A History. Random House/Rolling Stone Press 1984.

Powell, Polly, and Lucy Peel. Fifties and Sixties Style. Chartwell Books 1988.

Rubin, Jerry. We Are Everywhere. Harper & Row 1971.

Sims, Patterson. The Whitney Museum of American Art: Selected Works from the Permanent Collection. Norton 1985.

Stambler, Irwin. The Encyclopedia of Rock and Roll. St. Martin's 1989.

Stern, Jane and Michael. Sixties People. Knopf 1990.

Von Schmidt, Eric. Baby, Let Me Follow You Down: The Illustrated Story of the Cambridge Folk Years. Anchor Books 1979.

Wolfe, Tom. The Kandy-Kolored Tangerine Flake Streamline Baby. Farrar Straus & Giroux 1965.

_____. The Electric Kool-Aid Acid Test. Farrar Straus & Giroux 1968.

INDEX

Abbey Road, 90, *90*
Abernathy, Ralph, 49
Abstract Expressionism, 76, 77
Acid rock, 112
Adler, Lou, 91, 92
Aldrin, Edwin "Buzz," *40*, 41
Altamont music festival, 94–95, *94*
Animals, the, 108, 109
Anti-war movement, *8, 9*, 28–29, 60–61, 65,
    67–71, *72*, 73
Apollo 11, 41
Armies of the Night (Mailer), 68
Armstrong, Neil, *39*, 41
Artime, Manuel, 15

Baez, Joan, 60 *61*, 79, 80, *81*, 82
Balin, Marty, 95
Barnett, Governor Ross, 47
Beach Boys, the, 90, 103–104, *104*, 105
Beatles, the, 84–86, *85, 87*, 88–90, 107, 108,
    109, *109*
Bellbottoms, 8, 108, 115
Berlin Wall, 16
Birth-control pill, 98
Black Muslim movement, 52
Black Panther Party, 55–56, 57
British Invasion, 86, 105, 108
Brown, Helen Gurley, 98–99, 100
Burdon, Eric, 109

Calley, Lieutenant William, 29
Carmichael, Stokely, 55, 56, *56*, 61
Castro, Fidel, 12, *13, 14*
Cher, *82*, 83
China, 12, 32–33
Chou En-Lai, 33
Civil rights movement, 44–56
    Birmingham, Alabama, 47–48, 50
    Civil Rights Act (1964), 47, 50
    Freedom Riders, 46, *46*
    Johnson, Lyndon, and, 50–51, 56
    Kennedy, John F., and, 45, 47
    Kennedy, Robert, and, 45–46, 50
    March on Washington, 49
    Montgomery Bus Boycott, 44
    protest outside Woolworth's, *45*
    Selma, Alabama, 51, *52*
Clark, Ramsey, 56
Cleaver, Eldridge, 55, 56
Clifford, Clark, 26, 27
Cold War, the, 12–18

Berlin crisis, 12, 16
Cuban missile crisis, 17–18
fallout shelters, 16
U2 crisis, 12–13
Collins, Mike, 41
Congress for Racial Equality (CORE), 55, 59
Connor, Bull, 48, 50
Cronkite, Walter, 27–28
Crouch, Stanley, 53, 54
Cuba, 12
    Bay of Pigs, 14–15, *15*
    Cuban Missile Crisis, 17–18
    Cuban revolution, 13–14, *13*
Czechoslovakia, invasion of, 36, *36–37*

Daley, Mayor Richard, 61, 69
Dayan, Moshe, 35
"Days of Rage," 73
de Gaulle, Charles, 61
De Kooning, Willem, 76, 78
Dellinger, David, 67, 70
Democratic National Convention (1968), 69–70,
    71, 72
Diem, Ngo Dinh, 19, 21
Dobrynin, Anatoly, 17
Drug culture, the, 65, 110–117
Dubcek, Alexander, 36
Duchamp, Marcel, 76–77, 78
Dylan, Bob, 9, 79, 80, *81*, 82–83, 84

Eisenhower, Dwight David, 19
Electric Kool-Aid Acid Test, The (Wolfe), 111
Elijah Muhammad, 52
Ellsberg, Daniel, 23–24
Epstein, Brian, 84, 85, 86, 89, 90, 107
Evers, Charles, 48
Evers, Medgar, 48, *49*

"Flower Power," 113
Folk music, 79–83
Folk rock, 83
Free Speech Movement, *58*, 59–60, *59*, 65
Freedom Riders, 46
Fugs, the, 68, 69

Gagarin, Yuri, 39
Ginsberg, Allen, 113, 115
Glenn, Jr., John, *38*, 39
Grateful Dead, the, 91, 112, 113, 115
Great Proletarian Cultural Revolution, 32–33
Greene, Alexander Plunket, 106, 108
Gromyko, Andrei, 17
Guevara, Ernesto "Che," 13, *14*, 73
Guthrie, Woody, 79, 80

Haber, Al, 57
Haight-Ashbury district, 110, 111, 113, 115–116
Hair, 117, *117*
Halberstam, David, 20, 23
Haley, Alex, 53
Hard Day's Night, A, 86, 88
Harrison, George, 89, 90
Hayden, Tom, 57, 58, 63
Hefner, Hugh, 101, *101, 102*
Hell's Angels, 94–95, *94*
Hendrix, Jimi, 92, *92*, 105
Hersch, Seymour, 29
Hippies, 65, 67, 68, 69, 89, 91, 93, 105,
    113–116
Ho Chi Minh, 20
Hoffman, Abbie, 59, 65, *65*, 68, *68*
Hog Farm Commune, 93, *95, 116*
Hootenanny, 82
House UnAmerican Activities Committee (HUAC),
    65, *67*
Hulett, John, 55
Humphrey, Hubert, 70
Hungary, invasion of (1956), 12

Jagger, Mick, 90, 91, *94*, 95, 106, 110
Jefferson Airplane, 91, 95
Johns, Jasper, 78
Johnson, Lyndon, 23, 26, 27, 28, 50–51, 56,
    61, 67
Joplin, Janis, 92, *92*

Kennedy, Jackie, 99
Kennedy, John F., *31*
    assassination of, 30
    Bay of Pigs, 14–15, *15*
    Berlin speech, 18
    and civil rights movement, 45, 47, 49
    and "missile gap," 12
    Vienna summit, 15–16, *18*
    and Vietnam, 21, 23
Kennedy, Robert, 70
    and civil rights movement, 45–46, 50
    and Cuban crisis, 15, 16–17
Kerr, Clark, 60
Kesey, Ken, 111–112, *111*
Khruschev, Nikita, 12, 13, 15–16, 59
King, Martin Luther, 44, *44*, 45, 47–48, *48*, 49,
    50, *50*, 51, *51*, 52, 55, 56, 61
Ku Klux Klan, 82
Krassner, Paul, 68
Kunen, James, 62, 63

Lansdale, General Edward, 20
Leary, Timothy, 69, 109, 110–111, *114*, 115

Index

Lennon, John, 84, 88, 89, 90
Lichtenstein, Roy, 76
Liu Shao-chi, 32
LSD, 110–111, 112, 113, 114

Magical Mystery Tour, 90, *90*
Maharishi Mahesh Yogi, 90, 109, *109*
Mailer, Norman, *67*, 68
Malcolm X, *51*, 52–53
   assassination of, 53, *53*
Mao Tse-Tung, 32, *33*
March on the Pentagon (1967), 67–68
Marcus, Greil, 85–86, 88, 95
Marijuana, 110
Max, Peter, 110
McCarthy, Eugene, 61, 68
McCartney, Paul, 89, 90, 91
McKissick, Floyd, 55
McNamara, Robert, 23, 26
Meredith, James, 46–47, *47*, *54*, 55
Merry Pranksters, 111
Miniskirt, 106, 107
Mods, 106, 107, 108
Monkees, the, 88, *88*
Monterey International Pop Festival (1967), 91–92, 105
Monterey Pop (Pennebaker), 91
Motherwell, Robert, 76

Nabokov, Vladimir, 41
Nassar, Gamal Abdel, 35
New Left, 57, 65
Newman, Barnett, 77–78
Newton, Huey, 55, 56
Nixon, Richard, 28–29, 64, 70
Novotny, Antonin, 46
Nuclear test-ban treaty, 18, 30

Oldham, Andrew, 91
One Flew Over the Cuckoo's Nest (Kesey), 111
Oswald, Lee Harvey, 30
Owsley, Augustus, 112, 115

Parks, Rosa, 44
Partisan Review, The, 89
Peace Corps, 57
Perry, Charles, 114, 115
Peter, Paul and Mary, *83*
Philips, John, 91
Pigasus, 69, 70
Pillbox hat, 99–100
Plastic Ono Band, 90
Playboy magazine, 100–102
Pollock, Jackson, 76, 77

Pop art, 76–78
Port Huron Statement, 58
Powers, Francis Gary, 12–13
Project Apollo, 39
Psychedelia. *See* LSD.

Quant, Mary, 100, 106, 108

Racial riots
   following King assassination, 56
   Watts (1965), 53–55
Rauschenberg, Robert, 78
Red Guards, 32–33, *33*
Redding, Otis, 92, 105
Ringo Starr, 85, 86, 89, 90, 107
Rock Festivals, 91–93, 113
Rockers, 107
Rolling Stones, the, 88, 94–95, *94*, 108, *108*
Rosenquist, James, 78
Rothko, Mark, 78
Rubin, Jerry, 65, *66*, 67, 68
Rudd, Mark, 62

San Francisco Human Be-In of 1967, 114–115
Savio, Mario, 60
Seale, Bobby, 55, 56
Seeger, Pete, 82, *82*
Sex and the Single Girl (Brown), 98–99
Sgt. Pepper's Lonely Hearts Club Band, 89, 109
Sheehan, Neil, 23
Shepard, Alan, 39
Simon, Paul, 91
Six Day War, the, *34*, 35
Smothers Brothers, 82
Sonny and Cher, 83
Soul On Ice (Cleaver), 55
Southern Christian Leadership Conference (SCLC), 44
Soviet Union, 12, 13. *See also* Khruschev, Nikita.
Space race, the, 39–41
Spock, Dr. Benjamin 67
Sputnik, 39
Steinem, Gloria, 105
Stevenson, Adlai, 14, 17
Student activism, 57–64, *57. See also* Antiwar movement.
   Berkeley, University of California at, 58–59, *58*
   Columbia University, 62–63, *62*
   Cornell University, 63
   Jackson State University, 64
   Kent State University, 63–64, *64*
   Students for a Democratic Society (SDS), 57–58
   worldwide, 1968, 61

Student Nonviolent Coordinating Committee (SNCC), 55, 60
Students for a Democratic Society (SDS), 57–58, 62, 64, 70–71, 73
Sullivan, Ed, 85, 86
Summer of Love, 65, 67, 89, 91, 110, 115–116
Surfing, 103–105, *104*, *105*
   music, 103–104, 105
   surfer movies, 105
Swinging London, 106–108, 115

Taylor, General Maxwell, 65
Telstar, 40
Tereshkova, Valentina, 40
Third World, 12
Thompson, Hunter S., 70
Tito, Josip Broz, 36
Townshend, Pete, 106
Trips Festival (San Francisco), 113
Twiggy, 99, 100, *100*
Tynan, Kenneth, 89

Vienna Summit, 15–16
Vietnam War, 19–29. *See also* Antiwar movement.
   Buddhist monks, protests of, *21*
   "credibility gap," 23
   My Lai Massacre, *28*, 29
   origins of, 19–20
   pacification programs, 25, 27
   protests and demonstrations, *8, 9, 19, 21, 22, 27, 59*
   "Tet Offensive," 26–27, *26*, 61
   Tonkin Gulf Resolution, 23, 24

Wallace, George, 50, 51, 52
Warhol, Andy, 76, *76*, 77
Watts riots, 53–55
Wavy Gravy, 93
Weathermen, the, 57, 71, 73
Westmoreland, General William C., 24, 26, 28
Who, the, 88, 106, 108
Wilson, Brian, 103
Wilson, Dennis, 103
Wolfe, Tom, 77, 85, 103, 106, 111, 113
Women, changing roles of, 98–100, *98, 99*
Woodstock Music and Art Fair (1969), *92*, 93, *95*
Wreckers, the, 70–71

Yippies, 65, 67, 68, 69, *71*
Yoko Ono, 90
Young, Andrew, 56
Young, Israel "Izzy," 80

Popular Songs

1960

"Theme from A Summer Place" (Percy Faith)
"The Twist" (Chubby Checker)
"Puppy Love" (Paul Anka)
"Cathy's Clown" (Everly Brothers)
"Only the Lonely" (Roy Orbison)
"Alley Oop" (Hollywood Argyles)
"Itsy Bitsy Teenie Weenie Yellow Polkadot Bikini"
  (Brian Hyland)
"Chain Gang" (Sam Cooke)
"Save the Last Dance for Me" (Drifters)
"Stay" (Zodiacs)
"Shop Around" (Miracles)
"It's Now or Never" (Elvis Presley)
"You're Sixteen" (Johnny Burnette)
"Devil or Angel" (Bobby Vee)

1961

"Where the Boys Are" (Connie Francis)
"Moon River" (Jerry Butler)
"Will You Still Love Me Tomorrow?" (Shirelles)
"Blue Moon" (Marcels)
"Runaway" (Del Shannon)
"Mother-in-Law" (Ernie K-Doe)
"Stand By Me" (Ben E. King)
"Tossin' and Turnin'" (Bobby Lewis)
"Quarter to Three" (Gary "U. S." Bonds)
"I Like It Like That" (Chris Kenner)
"Take Good Care of My Baby" (Bobby Vee)
"Runaround Sue" (Dion)
"Hit the Road, Jack" (Ray Charles)
"Please Mr. Postman" (Marvelettes)
"Peppermint Twist" (Joey Dee & The Starlighters)
"Surrender" (Elvis Presley)
"Let's Twist Again" (Chubby Checker)
"Hello Mary Lou" (Ricky Nelson)
"Crying" (Roy Orbison)
"Calendar Girl" (Neil Sedaka)
"Spanish Harlem" (Ben E. King)

1962

"Duke of Earl" (Gene Chandler)
"The Lion Sleeps Tonight" (Tokens)
"Johnny Angel" (Shelly Fabares)
"She Cried" (Jay & the Americans)
"I Can't Stop Loving You" (Ray Charles)
"Palisades Park" (Freddy Cannon)
"Breaking Up Is Hard to Do" (Neil Sedaka)
"Loco-Motion" (Little Eva)
"Sherry" (The Four Seasons)
"Monster Mash" (Bobby "Boris" Pickett)
"He's a Rebel" (Crystals)
"Town Without Pity" (Gene Pitney)
"Limbo Rock" (Chubby Checker)
"Up on the Roof" (Drifters)
"Big Girls Don't Cry" (Four Seasons)
"Soldier Boy" (Shirelles)
"The Wah-Watusi" (Orlons)
"Surfer's Stomp" (Marketts)
"Return to Sender" (Elvis Presley)
"Surfin' Safari" (Beach Boys)
"If I Had a Hammer" (Peter, Paul & Mary)

1963

"Surfin' USA" (Beach Boys)
"It's My Party" (Leslie Gore)
"Blowin' in the Wind" (Peter, Paul & Mary)
"Surf City" (Jan and Dean)
"My Boyfriend's Back" (Angels)
"Walk Like a Man" (Four Seasons)

"Devil in Disguise" (Elvis Presley)
"Surfer Girl" (Beach Boys)
"Quicksand" (Martha and the Vandellas)
"Our Day Will Come" (Ruby and the Romantics)
"Wipe Out" (Surfaris)
"Blue Velvet" (Bobby Vinton)
"Da Doo Ron Ron" (Crystals)
"Puff the Magic Dragon" (Peter, Paul & Mary)
"Hey Paula" (Paul & Paula)
"He's So Fine" (Chiffons)
"Sugar Shack" (Jimmy Gilmer & the Fireballs)
"Be My Baby" (Ronettes)
"Louie Louie" (Kingsmen)

1964

"I Want To Hold Your Hand" (Beatles)
"She Loves You" (Beatles)
"Can't Buy Me Love" (Beatles)
"Twist and Shout" (Beatles)
"A Hard Day's Night" (Beatles)
"Glad All Over" (Dave Clark Five)
"Time Is On My Side" (Rolling Stones)
"She's Not There" (Zombies)
"How Do You Do It?" (Gerry & the Pacemakers)
"Rag Doll" (Four Seasons)
"My Guy" (Mary Wells)
"Walk On By" (Dionne Warwick)
"A World Without Love" (Peter & Gordon)
"I Get Around" (Beach Boys)
"Under the Boardwalk" (Drifters)
"Where Did Our Love Go?" (Supremes)
"House of the Rising Sun" (Animals)
"Do Wah Diddy Diddy" (Manfred Mann)
"Dancing in the Street" (Martha and the Vandellas)
"Oh, Pretty Woman" (Roy Orbison)
"Leader of the Pack" (Shangri-Las)
"Baby Love" (Supremes)
"You Really Got Me" (Kinks)
"The Little Old Lady (From Pasadena)" (Jan and Dean)
"I'm Into Something Good" (Herman's Hermits)
"Fun, Fun, Fun" (Beach Boys)
"Chapel of Love" (Dixie Cups)
"Love Potion No. 9" (Searchers)
"A World Without Love" (Peter and Gordon)
"Baby, I Need Your Loving" (Four Tops)

1965

"Ticket to Ride" (Beatles)
"Help!" (Beatles)
"We Can Work It Out" (Beatles)
"Day Tripper" (Beatles)
"Yesterday" (Beatles)
"Downtown" (Petula Clark)
"Get Off of My Cloud" (Rolling Stones)
"You've Lost That Lovin' Feelin'" (Righteous Brothers)
"What the World Needs Now Is Love" (Jackie De
  Shannon)
"Help Me Rhonda" (Beach Boys)
"Goin' Out of My Head" (Little Anthony and the
  Imperials)
"Go Now" (Moody Blues)
"Do You Believe in Magic" (Lovin' Spoonful)
"For Your Love" (Yardbirds)
"In the Midnight Hour" (Wilson Pickett)
"Stop! In the Name of Love" (Supremes)
"It's Not Unusual" (Tom Jones)
"California Girls" (Beach Boys)
"Turn! Turn! Turn!" (Byrds)
"Tracks of My Tears" (Miracles)
"Catch Us If You Can" (Dave Clark Five)
"Positively Fourth Street" (Bob Dylan)
"We've Got to Get Out of This Place" (Animals)
"Ferry 'Cross the Mersey" (Gerry & the Pacemakers)
"My Girl" (Temptations)

"King of the Road" (Roger Miller)
"Game of Love" (Mindbenders)
"Mrs. Brown You've Got a Lovely Daughter"
  (Herman's Hermits)
"I Can't Help Myself" (Four Tops)
"Mr. Tambourine Man" (Byrds)
"Woolly Bully" (Sam the Sham & the Pharaohs)
"(I Can't Get No) Satisfaction" (Rolling Stones)
"Like a Rolling Stone" (Bob Dylan)
"I Got You, Babe" (Sonny & Cher)
"Papa's Got a Brand New Bag" (James Brown)
"Hang On Sloopy" (McCoys)
"Rescue Me" (Fontella Bass)

1966

"Eleanor Rigby" (Beatles)
"Paperback Writer" (Beatles)
"California Dreamin'" (Mamas and the Papas)
"Sounds of Silence" (Simon & Garfunkel)
"Summer in the City" (Lovin' Spoonful)
"Lightnin' Strikes" (Lou Christie)
"These Boots Are Made for Walkin'" (Nancy Sinatra)
"Paint It Black" (Rolling Stones)
"My Generation" (Who)
"Cherish" (Association)
"Eight Miles High" (Byrds)
"Last Train to Clarksville" (Monkees)
"Uptight" (Stevie Wonder)
"The Ballad of the Green Berets" (Sgt. Barry Sadler)
"Wild Thing" (Troggs)
"Bus Stop" (Hollies)
"96 Tears" (? and the Mysterians)
"Walk Away Renee" (Left Banke)
"19th Nervous Breakdown" (Rolling Stones)
"You Can't Hurry Love" (Supremes)
"A Groovy Kind of Love" (Mindbenders)
"Time Won't Let Me" (Outsiders)
"Reach Out I'll Be There" (Four Tops)
"What Becomes of the Brokenhearted" (Jimmy Ruffin)
"Good Vibrations" (Beach Boys)
"When a Man Loves a Woman" (Percy Sledge)
"Just Like a Woman" (Bob Dylan)
"King of a Drag" (Buckinghams)
"Winchester Cathedral" (New Vaudeville Band)

1967

"Light My Fire" (Doors)
"All You Need Is Love" (Beatles)
"Whiter Shade of Pale" (Procol Harum)
"Let's Spend the Night Together" (Rolling Stones)
"Incense and Peppermints" (Strawberry Alarm Clock)
"Mellow Yellow" (Donovan)
"Penny Lane" (Beatles)
"Strawberry Fields Forever" (Beatles)
"Purple Haze" (Jimi Hendrix)
"People Are Strange" (Doors)
"I Think We're Alone Now" (Tommy James and the
  Shondells)
"Brown-Eyed Girl" (Van Morrison)
"I Second that Emotion" (Miracles)
"Never My Love" (Association)
"San Francisco" (Scott McKenzie)
"59th Street Bridge Song" (Harper's Bizarre)
"White Rabbit" (Jefferson Airplane)
"Gimme Some Lovin'" (Spencer Davis Group)
"I Can See for Miles" (Who)
"Happy Together" (Turtles)
"Groovin'" (Young Rascals)
"Georgy Girl" (Seekers)
"Respect" (Aretha Franklin)
"Ode to Billie Joe" (Bobbie Gentry)
"Can't Take My Eyes Off of You" (Frankie Valli)
"The Letter" (Box Tops)
"For What It's Worth" (Buffalo Springfield)

"To Sir With Love" (Lulu)
"Soul Man" (Sam & Dave)
"Different Drum" (Linda Ronstadt & the Stone Poneys)
"There's a Kind of Hush" (Herman's Hermits)
"This Diamond Ring" (Gary Lewis)
"Ruby Tuesday" (Rolling Stones)

1968

"Hey Jude" (Beatles)
"Revolution" (Beatles)
"Born To Be Wild" (Steppenwolf)
"Green Tambourine" (Lemon Pipers)
"Hello I Love You" (Doors)
"Love Is Blue" (Paul Mauriat)
"Dock of the Bay" (Otis Redding)
"In-a-Gadda-Da-Vida" (Iron Butterfly)
"Crimson and Clover" (Tommy James and the
  Shondells)
"MacArthur Park" (Richard Harris)
"Jumpin' Jack Flash" (Rolling Stones)
"This Guy's in Love with You" (Herb Alpert)
"For Once in My Life" (Stevie Wonder)
"Love Is All Around" (Troggs)
"I Heard It Through the Grapevine" (Marvin Gaye)
"Mrs. Robinson" (Simon & Garfunkel)
"Abraham, Martin and John" (Dion)
"Stoned Soul Picnic" (Fifth Dimension)
"Piece of My Heart" (Janis Joplin)
"Judy in Disguise (With Glasses)" (John Fred and His
  Playboy Band)
"Both Sides Now" (Judy Collins)
"Young Girl" (Union Gap)
"Lady Madonna" (Beatles)
"Tighten Up" (Archie Bell & the Drells)
"Yummy Yummy Yummy" (Ohio Express)
"People Got To Be Free" (Rascals)
"Sunshine of Your Love" (Cream)
"Girl Watcher" (O'Kaysions)
"Magic Bus" (Who)
"Midnight Confession" (Grass Roots)
"Bend Me, Shape Me" (American Breed)

1969

"Time of the Season" (Zombies)
"Everyday People" (Sly & the Family Stone)
"Proud Mary" (Creedence Clearwater Revival)
"Honky Tonk Woman" (Rolling Stones)
"Suspicious Minds" (Elvis Presley)
"Alice's Restaurant" (Arlo Guthrie)
"Sugar Sugar" (Archies)
"Okie from Muskogee" (Merle Haggard)
"Aquarius/Let the Sunshine In" (Fifth Dimension)
"Touch Me" (Doors)
"In the Year 2525" (Zager & Evans)
"A Boy Named Sue" (Johnny Cash)
"Hooked On a Feeling" (B. J. Thomas)
"Magic Carpet Ride" (Steppenwolf)
"It's Your Thing" (Isley Brothers)
"Get Back" (Beatles)
"Lay Lady Lay" (Bob Dylan)
"Something" (Beatles)
"Build Me Up Buttercup" (Foundations)
"Whole Lotta Love" (Led Zeppelin)
"Crystal Blue Persuasion" (Tommy James and the
  Shondells)
"Hair" (Cowsills)
"Pinball Wizard" (Who)
"Give Peace a Chance" (John Lennon/Plastic Ono Band)
"Someday We'll Be Together" (Supremes)
"In the Ghetto" (Elvis Presley)
"Good Morning Starshine" (Oliver)
"Put a Little Love in Your Heart" (Jackie De Shannon)
"I Want You Back" (Jackson Five)
"Everybody's Talkin'" (Nilsson)